contents

Foreword by Ian Hislop
Author's Introduction

PRE-WAR [10]

1914 *Mons – Christmas truce* [47]

1915 *Neuve Chapelle – Gallipoli* [75]

1916 *Verdun – The Somme* [113]

1917 *Arras – Cambrai* [179]

1918 *Picardy – Armistice* [237]

AFTERMATH [273]

index [284]
acknowledgements [286]

foreword

MAX ARTHUR has already done a great deal to recover the forgotten voices of the First World War. Now he has added the faces to go with them. Unlike him, I am not an expert on the War but I do know why this latest collection is so important. In a series of television programmes called *Not Forgotten* I tried to bring back to life a few of the endless names of the First World War dead that are listed on the nations' war memorials. We started with the stone inscription and then tried to flesh out the stories with documents, memories of relatives and of course with pictures. And this was the always the key. We were desperate to find photographs because once you had an image, however grainy or faded, then suddenly the figure was not just another grim statistic but a human being. And that is why this book is so compelling. For there in far off black-and-white-land are our fathers, grandfathers, and great grandfathers. There beneath the tin helmets and behind the moustaches are men not so very different from ourselves, put in situations which we find it almost impossible to imagine. Here their faces tell the story of the war from the naive enthusiasm of 1914 through to the battered relief of 1918 with all the suffering and the misery in between. There are pictures taken at Ypres, The Somme, Passchendale, Cambrai, Gallipoli and all the other major battles in the familiar roll-call of horror. If it is tempting sometimes to think that we know all about the First World War and that the images of the conflict have become clichés and have lost

their power to move us, this collection proves otherwise. All those individual faces staring out at us nearly a century later: faces under top hats or flat caps, in balaclavas or bandages, in gas masks or goggles, registering all the emotions of ordinary men living through an extraordinary war. There is pain and tragedy and exhaustion but there is also camaraderie and courage and stoicism. How often do the men smile at the camera when, to our eyes, there can be so little to smile about? The trench newspaper the *Wipers Times* jokingly described this condition as "suffering from cheerfulness". Wilfred Owen gave a memorable description of what he called "faces grimly gay".

Because there is no escape here from the face of death, Max Arthur does not spare us the photographs of corpses and unlike the civilian population of the time we are not to be protected from pictures of the dead. It is interesting that one such image shows a row of bodies where the faces have been covered in preparation for burial as if even on the battlefield this sight were unbearable. But such delicacy is not observed elsewhere and we are shown plenty of dead faces, including one that has rotted away to a skull whilst still inside a uniform. It looks like an awful memento mori in an old painting.

And in a sense that is the point of this remarkable collection, a sobering reminder of death in war, yet it is also an engaging act of remembrance of the lives of all those caught up in it – a tribute to all the forgotten faces.

Ian Hislop

introduction

IN FORGOTTEN VOICES OF THE GREAT WAR I tried to capture the human drama of the war in the words of the soldiers and civilians who endured those five fateful years.

Now, in *The Faces Of World War I*, I have tried, through photographs to capture the enduring spirit of the soldier and civilian. I have wherever possible, followed the war on the Western Front and at Gallipoli, chronologically through its major battles. It has not, however, always been possible to put the photographs in date order. What the photographs show is the build-up to an attack, the men in the trenches, readying themselves for battle, then going over the top. There are very few action shots. Photographers, brave as they were, were not to be seen taking photographs of soldiers advancing towards them over no-man's-land.

I have also attempted to portray everyday life in the trenches, as well as aspects of the war that are rarely seen, including Zulu warriors on the Western Front; soldiers dressed as women preparing to appear on stage; regimental sports days and fraternisation between enemy soldiers.

Images from the post-war period bear witness to the nature of the terrible injuries the men sustained – and the efforts of the medical profession to restore some dignity and quality of life to the war-scarred survivors.

The quotations accompanying many of the photographs come from the men – and women – who lived through this war. More than just captions, they press home the rawness of the human experience that is depicted in these pages.

I have tried throughout to capture the spirit of the soldier on both sides, but not only his spirit, also his humour, his ability to endure, his sense of defiance and his courage to withstand the often appalling conditions. Some images will inevitably be disturbing – but this was the reality of life on the front line. There are some photographs which follow no particular theme, but simply capture a poignant moment. There are photographs in this book, taken from private collections, which have never been seen before in print. Others are classic shots of the war. I hope I have struck a balance.

Max Arthur
London, 2007

TITANIC
DISASTER
GREAT LOSS
OF LIFE
EVENING NEWS

A MAN WITH A HANDFUL OF PAWN TICKETS sits with his family in London's East End, July 1912. Poverty was endemic in Pre-First World War Britain. Over 40 per cent of those enlisting in 1914 were found to be malnourished during their medical examinations.

A GROUP OF PLAYERS of the Eton wall game, c.1912. In common with many of the other public schools of the era, Eton provided a substantial number of recruits for the British Army. A total number of 1,157 Old Etonians were killed during the course of the war.

DESPITE ABJECT POVERTY, a great camaraderie, humour and defiance was apparent in the tenements and backyards. The vast majority of the British Army came from urban or agricultural working class families.

IN A GAS-LIT PARLOUR, a wife washes her husband's back as he sits in a
tin bath. The house had no bathroom and the toilet was outside.

TWO OF THE ETON COLLEGE cricket team are accompanied back to the pavilion during the 1909 Eton vs Harrow match at Lords. Of the Harrow team, four of the players were to die on the Western front: A.H. Lang *was killed in action at Ginchy, 25 January 1915*; T.L.G. Turnbull *died of wounds near St Eloi, 15 April*, G.W.V. Hopley *died of wounds at Boulogne 12 May 1915*; T. B. Wilson *was killed at Ypres, 18 July 1917.*

Of the Eton team: Hon. A. Windsor-Clive *was killed in action at Landrecies, 25 August 1914*; J. Kekewitch *was killed at Loos, 29 September 1915*; Hon. V.D. Boscawen *was killed at Gheluvelt, 27 May 1918.* Seven of the twenty-two players who took the field that day were dead by June 1918.

THE BRITISH AND GERMAN ARMIES were structured quite differently in the years preceding the outbreak of war. The German Army was not a single unitary army but an army of four kingdoms, Bavaria, Prussia, Saxony and Württemburg, constructed on the same lines as the army that had defeated the Austrians in 1866 and the French in 1870.

GERMAN CIVILIANS and (*overleaf*) soldiers posing for the camera in the carefree days before the war.

IN GERMANY, (*opposite*) all men between the ages of 17 and 45 were eligible
for military service, spending the ages of 17 to 22 in the Landsturm, (a home defence
force) before progressing to either the Standing or Supplementary Reserve armies.
The German army had a reserve of 4.3 million trained men.

Above

AT THE OUTBREAK OF WAR THE British Army was a small, professional force of
247,000 soldiers, of which half was serving overseas in the British Empire. This army was
supported by 224,000 recruits and 269,000 Territorials.

" ONE SENSED A TREMENDOUS expectancy of war in
the near future. A favourite bestselling book was
Welmacht Oder Untergang ('World Domination or
Decline'). "

William Ewen, an English student in Berlin

THE REGULAR FORCES of the British Army were bolstered by a
new formation – the Territorial Force, which was formed in 1908 to
serve as a home defence force. On the outbreak of World War I,
many Territorial battalions volunteered for service in France. Here,
outside a recruiting office, an officer sits with soldiers past and
future, keen to "do their bit".

CRISIS IN SARAJEVO. The Archduke Franz Ferdinand was the second in line to the throne of Austria-Hungary. His assassination on 28 June 1914 during a visit to Sarajevo in the province of Bosnia and Herzegovina provoked Austria-Hungary into a confrontation with Serbia, which would lead to the outbreak of World War I.

THE ASSASSIN, a young Bosnian, named Gavrilo Princip (centre, with his two co-conspirators) was part of the "Young Bosnia" movement that sought to join the Austro-Hungarian province of Bosnia and Herzegovina with the independent Slavic state of Serbia. It was this perceived Serbian interest and support that ultimately led to Austria-Hungary's declaration of war.

A PROCLAMATION, declaring the start of war in Europe,
posted up in Whitehall.

A YOUNG BOY among the workers, leaving a manufacturing
company in 1909. He would have been of fighting age by 1914.
Many under-aged boys joined up for the prospect of adventure,
expecting the war to be over by Christmas.

THE POLITICAL INSTABILITY following the assassination was reflected in Europe's financial centres. The London Stock Exchange closed at the end of July 1914, not opening again until early 1915. Some of those who worked there formed the Stock Exchange Battalion of Royal Fusiliers – out of 1,600 who volunteered, 400 never returned.

A BERLIN CROWD listens as a German officer reads the Kaiser's order for mobilization on 1 August 1914. A year later the Kaiser declared:

" I look upon the people and the nation as handed on to me as a responsibility conferred upon me by God, and I believe, as it is written in the Bible, that it is my duty to increase this heritage for which one day I shall be called upon to give an account. Whoever tries to interfere with my task I shall crush. "

PRE-WAR

- EDWARDIAN BRITAIN

- PRE-WAR GERMANY

- THE LANDSTURM AND THE GERMAN ARMY

- BRITISH RESERVES AND REGULARS

- CRISIS IN EUROPE AND DECLARATION
  OF WAR

- MOBILIZATION AND MILITARIZATION

ONE OF THE MOST EVOCATIVE *images of the Titanic disaster is the photo of a young boy selling the* Evening News *outside the White Star offices in Cockspur Street, London. This young boy was Ned Parfett whose own life was to end tragically. He enlisted in the Royal Artillery in 1916 and was awarded the Military Medal for bravery before he was killed a fortnight before the end of the war. He is buried at Verchain-Maugré in France.*

PLAYERS' FAMILIES arriving at the Eton vs Harrow cricket match, Lords Cricket Ground, 1914.

MEN ENLISTED FOR a variety of reasons. Some genuinely felt the patriotic urge to do their bit for king and country, others sought the excitement of the army as a change from the daily routine of dull, poorly paid jobs. As part of the recruitment process the recruits were give a perfunctory medical examination to check for any obvious defects in eyesight, teeth and chest. The eyesight test is shown here.

" THE SERGEANT said to me, 'Get on the scales.' He weighed me, took my height and said, 'Now we'll go round to the doctor for a medical exam.' The doctor told me to take all my clothes off, which embarrassed me very much. "

S. C. Lang

UPON THE OUTBREAK OF WAR the newly appointed
Secretary of State for War, Lord Kitchener, had appealed
for volunteers to bolster Britain's small Regular Army.
The initial response was overwhelming with more than
1,186,000 volunteers enlisting in the first five months of
the war. These men needed to be trained and a network
of depots and camps were set up throughout the country.
Here at Mychett Camp in Farnborough Cambridge
University students are being shown how to use the
.303 Lee Enfield rifle.

❝ I HAD ONE YEAR UP AT CAMBRIDGE and then
volunteered for the Army. We were quite clear
that Germany would be defeated by 7 October
when we would go back to Cambridge. ❞

Private Godfrey Buxton, RAMC

RECRUITS OF ETON College Officers Training Corps drilling during Recruit Week. The major public schools provided a large number of recruits for Kitchener's New Armies, both as officers and in the ranks.

❝ DURING OUR TRAINING in Crowborough in Sussex it was a month of great heat – we sweated tremendously. We carried about 60lb of ammunition, kit and our rifle. We got blisters, but we did about 15 or 16 miles a day, with ten minutes' halt every hour. We lay on our backs gasping, water bottles were drunk dry. ❞

Henry Williamson, London Rifle Brigade

RECRUITS OF THE "GRIMSBY CHUMS", the 10th Battalion, The Lincolnshire Regiment, at rifle drill during their training. Like all "Pals" the Grimsby Chums was made up of men who lived and worked side by side. The "Grimsby chums" were formed by the former headmaster of Winteringham Secondary School. They were assured that they would fight side by side. Today, as the final image of the book shows, they lie side by side.

IN GERMANY soldiers march to the train station. Here, one is accompanied by his wife who helps him carry his pack.

IN BRITAIN an Expeditionary Force of four infantry divisions and five cavalry brigades was assembled to be despatched to the Continent where it would take its place on the left of the line of French Armies. This force was made up of regular soldiers, bolstered by a large number of reservists re-called for the duration of hostilities.

WESTMINSTER FUSILIERS (*above*) wait for their troop train at Waterloo Station, London, during mobilization while (*opposite*) the British Expeditionary Force leaves for the front.

" GOODBYE DOLLY I must leave you though it breaks my heart to go, something tells me I am needed at the front to fight the foe… "

Popular song of the period

1914

- BRITISH EXPEDITIONARY FORCE ARRIVES IN FRANCE
- MONS: ADVANCE AND WITHDRAWAL
- FIRST BATTLE OF THE MARNE
- FIRST BATTLE OF YPRES, MESSINES
- CHRISTMAS TRUCE

BELGIAN REFUGEES WITH BRITISH TROOPS *in the background, on the retreat from Mons.*

IN THE GLORIOUS SUNSHINE OF JUNE 1914 there was no thought of war, no international crisis and no hint that the crowned heads of Europe were poised to tumble one after the other. The assassination of the heir to the Austro-Hungarian Empire on 28 June was neither predictable nor inevitable. Yet within weeks, millions of men were on the march.

The assassination of Archduke Franz Ferdinand was blamed on the Serbs by Austria-Hungary and on 6 July the German government confirmed that it would support Austria-Hungary in reprisals against the Serbs. The First World War might have ended as a localized Balkan war except for two factors: Imperial Germany's ambition to supersede Great Britain as the world's superpower (and Britain's desire to retain her position), and a complex series of treaties that locked countries together with promises of mutual support in the event of war.

On 24 July, Serbia appealed for help to Russia and two days later Austria-Hungary declared war on Serbia. At the end of July, Russia, linked by treaty to France, began to mobilize. Germany presented ultimatums to Russia and France threatening war if they did not

demobilize. On 1 August, Germany declared war on Russia and a day later German soldiers entered the tiny principality of Luxembourg. On 3 August, Germany declared war on France and, the following day, its troops marched into neutral Belgium. Britain immediately issued an ultimatum to Germany and, as it was ignored, she formally declared war on the same day.

Germany's move into Belgium was in accordance with the "Schlieffen Plan". This was a carefully constructed strategy which anticipated a war on two fronts – against France in the west and Russia in the east. German forces would first invade France through Belgium and then march towards Paris in a circular motion. This manoeuvre would take the French Army by surprise, allowing for a quick victory which would then allow the German Army to redeploy its troops on the Eastern Front against the Russians. The entire endeavour was expected to bring victory over the French within six weeks.

It was in reaction to the invasion of Belgium that the main body of the British Army was shipped to France. Unlike their allies and enemies, recruited by mass conscription, the British had a small professional army of volunteers; even with the recently created (1908) Territorial Force and all the reserves mobilized, the British had around 710,000 men, of whom 247,000 were regulars. France, prepared since 1871 for another war with Germany, had 823,000 men under arms in 1914; by the end of August they were reinforced by some 2,870,000 reservists reporting for duty. For all the excellence of their pre-war training and vastly higher standards, the six British infantry divisions could make little strategic difference to the 1914 campaign in western Europe. France had 62 divisions; Germany fielded 87; Russia had 114. There was a rush to recruiting offices as thousands of young men were

❝ There was a rush to recruiting offices as thousands of young men were drawn to join their pals in a challenging adventure. ❞

drawn by patriotism and a desire to join their pals in a challenging adventure that would prove their manhood. There was also a conviction that the war would be quick and would be "Over by Christmas".

As the British Expeditionary Force (BEF) was disembarking in France in August, the French were launching an all-out offensive to recapture the provinces of Alsace and Lorraine, annexed by Germany after the war of 1870. Unwittingly the French were playing into the hands of their opponents; the German First and Second Armies swept in a wide arc through Belgium and into France, intent on swinging around to seize Paris and strike the main French armies from the flank and rear. The German forces – four armies advancing through Belgium and another through Luxembourg – set out on August 4th and it had been expected, among German planners, that Belgium would capitulate without a fight, allowing their advance to proceed unhindered. However, King Albert of the Belgians decided to fight, and the modern fortifications around Liège and Namur seriously delayed the German push. Only by bringing up their heavy artillery and shelling the fortifications into submission could the German Army breakthrough, with Liège falling on 16 August and Namur a week later.

As the French First and Second Armies advanced into Alsace, the German Sixth and Seventh armies fell back before them, but the front stabilized on 18 August and the Germans counter-attacked along the entire front, driving the French back to where they had started, along the river Meurthe. In the forested area of the Ardennes, too, the French Third and Fourth Armies met stiff resistance, and the Fifth Army, with the BEF, pressed on into Belgium to confront the spearheads of the German First Army.

The first major action involving the British Expeditionary Force took place on 23 August amid the slagheaps and pitheads of the coalfields at Mons. On the previous day the French Fifth Army had been forced back, so Field Marshal Sir John French, commanding the BEF, promised to take action to hold the Germans up for twenty-four hours to buy the French time to regroup. The BEF was a small force of tough well-trained professional soldiers, and they went into action against superior German numbers: seventy thousand British troops with three hundred guns faced a hundred and sixty thousand Germans with six hundred guns.

The outnumbered British regulars gave the German Army a bloody nose before withdrawing. The casualty figures were 1,600 British to 5,000 Germans – a tribute to the fighting quality of the regular soldiers. It was reckoned that the British infantrymen could fire fifteen rounds a minute with their Lee Enfield rifles, leading the Germans to believe that they were being fired on by machine guns. In the retreat that followed, in which many Belgian refugees were caught up (see *opposite*) the British and French armies withdrew to the River Marne, provoking the German Army to turn west of Paris rather than to the east as was their original plan. The Allied forces were retreating at a rate of some twenty miles a day. Their commander, General Joffre, jettisoned pre-war strategy and reorganized his forces for a counter-strike on the approaches to Paris. Feeling the pressure of the German advance, the French government left Paris on the 2nd September and on the 6th the First Battle of the Marne began. The River Marne is south of the Aisne and to the east of Paris, and the battle was fought on a line from Compiègne to Verdun. The Germans were initially pushed back by the reorganized Allied forces. As the German armies withdrew, the Allies pursued them to the River Aisne, where, on 13 September, the German positions were assaulted by the French 5th and 6th Armies, with the BEF in their centre, and although the 6th crossed the river with the help of a pontoon bridge and secured the north bank, they were driven back by a counter-attack and no further progress was made. General von Moltke, the German Commander-in-Chief, had lost control of his army commanders. Once the armies had outrun their telephone lines, he attempted to command by radio from his remote headquarters, but the temperamental machinery broke down and the French listening post atop the Eiffel Tower monitored the transmissions. Eventually, Moltke sent one of his staff officers to drive between the German Army commanders to order them to fall back to defensive positions if necessary. After the battle, von Moltke was replaced as Commander-in Chief of the German Army by General von Falkenhayn.

Germany's grand strategy had failed. German and Allied forces then raced northwards towards the Channel, attempting to find an open flank, and by October the Western Front had reached the sea. The fluid frontline of August and September congealed all the way to the North Sea, leaving the rival armies confronting each other along 460 continuous miles. As winter set in, rain turned the low-lying ground of Flanders into a brown mush. Churned up by shell-fire, the mud was so deep and glutinous that men drowned in it. Both sides dug in as best they could. The participants became locked into trench warfare.

The Germans were in fortunate possession of the higher, drier ground, on which they built concrete blockhouses; the British, less well placed, worked frantically to improve their trenches and keep them clear of water by pumps but even so, often had to stand for hours knee-deep in water. Along all sections of the front, the soon-to-be familiar accompaniments of trench warfare arrived. These were lice, fleas, bugs, rats, trench-foot (a form of foot rot which can be fatal and is always incapacitating), trench fever, fatigue, decomposing and unburied bodies, rudimentary hygiene and perpetual damp, as well as pneumonia and all the ailments that inevitably accompany exposure. Both sides set up barbed-wire defences under cover of darkness; usually parties from each side crawled out on a following night to cut through them in preparation for raids or a forthcoming attack, or to take prisoners in order to gain information about the enemy's preparations.

These field fortifications came to dominate fighting on the Western Front and restricted the scope for manoeuvre by all sides, though many attempts were made by both sides to penetrate the enemy's lines. The final great western offensive of 1914 took place at the end of November, when the BEF, and in particular I Corps under Sir Douglas Haig, stood in the way of an assault organized by von Falkenhayn to break through to Dunkirk and Calais. The German Fourth and Sixth Armies streamed forward towards Ypres, but were held up by the disciplined rifle fire of the BEF. The German advance was halted but the British were left in an exposed salient, dominated on three sides by German forces and subject to incessant artillery fire.

On Christmas Day, fighting stopped on the Western Front and tentative contact was made between the two sides in no-man's-land. The front-line soldiers had a great deal in common and the informal truce lasted for most of the day until the troops were ordered back into their trenches. On the same day, the world's first carrier-launched air strike took place when the Royal Naval Air Service bombed the Cuxhaven naval base in northern Germany.

Although three German corps were diverted from France to the Eastern Front for the struggle against Russia, it was clear that the main theatre of war would remain the Western Front. While Germany was obliged to stiffen its Austro-Hungarian allies with increasing numbers of divisions, the main body of the German Army remained in France and Belgium, facing the British and French.

" The fluid front line congealed all the way to the North Sea, leaving rival armies confronting each other along 400 miles. "

Just four months before, at the start of the war, Germany had amassed its forces almost exclusively on the Western Front, in an attempt to defeat France and Britain quickly before concentrating on the war against Russia. Only ten divisions of the German Eighth Army had been left on the Eastern Front and they were forced to withstand a major Russian assault despite being outnumbered by two to one. The German high command made two new appointments – Hindenburg as Commander-in-Chief of the Eighth Army, and Ludendorff as Chief of Staff. Shrewd military tacticians, they took advantage of the historical antipathy between the commanders of the two Russian Armies. These two forces were becoming increasingly separated during the long advance into East Prussia, and Hindenberg and Ludendorff transported men in by train to confront the Russian Second Army, eventually surrounding and defeating them at Tannenberg at the end of August. Over the course of four days, 90,000

Russians were captured and 18,000 killed. In early September the Russian First Army was driven back – the Battle of the Masurian Lakes was the last time a Russian Army would fight on German soil during the conflict. The Russian assault had largely been made at the behest of the French to divert forces from the Western Front – and it had certainly done that, weakening the right wing of the German assault in the west.

The first winter of the war found the troops in deadlock on the Western Front, and as the year drew to an end, in the freezing cold and endless mud of the trenches, Christmas had come and gone but the war was not "All Over."

Below
British new recruits march alongside armed officers, following the outbreak of war.

" THE JOURNEY ACROSS was peaceful. We had no escort – nothing. When we got there, we camped for about three or four days, then we went and trained at Le Havre, and then it was up to the Front. We went on a cattle-truck type train, eight horses and forty men. "

Fusilier William Holbrook

Above

BRITISH TROOPS and horses cross the Channel aboard a troopship.

Opposite

BRITISH TROOPS ASLEEP on Boulogne Quay, having just arrived to join their French and Belgian allies.

Below

CURIOUS FRENCH CIVILIANS watch two kilted Scottish soldiers (*below*). The French gave a warm welcome to the BEF as they arrived to support their troops.

Opposite

BRITISH SOLDIERS, newly arrived in France, preparing to go to the lines, not knowing what a precarious situation they faced, August 1914.

" BEFORE WE GOT TO MONS, we went through a place called Frameries, a
mining town about ten miles from Mons. It was wonderful there – the people
came out and cheered and shouted and gave us food, and a tremendous
welcome. "

Fusilier William Holbrook

THE VAST ARMY that the BEF was to meet head-on is seen here, as German infantry advance in formation over open country.

“ WE MARCHED ON AND ON. We never dared take off our boots, because our feet were so swollen that we didn't think it would be possible to put them on again. In one small village the mayor came and asked our company commanders not to allow us to cut off the hands of children. These were atrocity stories he had heard about us. ”

Sergeant Stefan Westmann, 29th Division, German Army

A COMPANY OF THE 4th Battalion Royal Fusiliers, resting in the Grand Place, Mons, 22 August, before the battle the following day, during which the battalion won two VCs (Lieutenant Dease and Private Godley) on the canal bridge at Vimy, two miles north of Mons.

Opposite
British and Belgian soldiers retreating from Mons.

❝ WE WERE VERY DISAPPOINTED when we were ordered to break up the battle and retreat, but we were thankful the Germans had withdrawn after this very severe battle, because we were feeling thoroughly tired. We were completely exhausted, thoroughly hungry, and I don't think we were capable of any reasonable further movement. There was only one thing that managed to keep us going, and that was the knowledge that we were fighting for our very lives. ❞

Gunner Walter Burchmore, Royal Horse Artillery

Opposite

HUSSARS AT THE END OF THE RETREAT – the cavalry had a day's rest at Gournay, near Paris, while the 11th Hussars were bivouacked in the grounds of Madame Townsend's chateau at Champs. This photo shows Lieutenant Arkwright, who was killed while flying later in the war.

“ **AFTER ADVANCING SEVERAL DAYS** into Belgium and passing these refugees, many of them with their little dogcarts and piled with their pitiful possessions, prams, children, one thing and another, we found ourselves eventually going the same way as the refugees, so we knew very well we were no longer advancing into Belgium. ”

Gunner J. W. Palmer, Royal Field Artillery.

BATTLE OF THE MARNE. The 1st Middlesex First-Line Transport struck by shrapnel at Signy Signets, 8 September 1914. Nine horses were killed and a watercart riddled. The man with the goggles belongs to the Intelligence Corps – he is badly wounded in the head.

“ WE WENT FORWARD as we had been trained. One section would advance under covering fire of another section, leapfrogging each other as the others were firing to keep Jerry's heads down. My company was going in with their bayonets when suddenly Jerry put up a white flag. We were really surprised. We took four hundred and fifty prisoners. I said to one of them, ‘Why did you pack up when you've got so much ammunition?’ He said, ‘Your fire was so accurate we couldn't put our heads up to shoot at you.’ We lost twelve, killed, and sixty wounded; they lost about a hundred and eighty men. ”

Sergeant Thomas Painting, 1st Battalion, King's Royal Rifle Corps

DEAD GERMAN SOLDIER from the First Battle of the Marne.

MEN OF THE OXFORD AND BUCKS Light Infantry sheltering from shrapnel behind the headquarters of the 20th Brigade, 7th Division, during the first battle of Ypres, October 1914.

Opposite
A PATROL OF the 2nd Battalion Gordon Highlanders waiting to go forward near Ypres, October 1914.

" WE COULD SEE A ROAD running towards Ypres from our hillside, and on it we saw a group of French soldiers. While we were watching, there was the sound of heavy gunfire and, after a few seconds, three violent explosions. When the smoke had cleared we saw this group picking up one of their number and immediately start to dig a grave for him, so the shell had killed him. That was the first time we realized what the war was about. **"**

Private Clifford Lane, 1st Battalion, Hertfordshire Regiment.

THE REMNANTS of the London Scottish after the Battle of Messines,
31 October 1914. The ridge was captured by the Germans, 1 November.

CAPTAIN MOORHOUSE, 2nd Argyll and Sutherland Highlanders, awaiting an opportunity to snipe at the Germans ranged opposite at Bois Grenier, November 1914.

A GROUP OF THE 1ST BATTALION London Rifle Brigade just
after dinner, Ploegsteert Wood, Christmas Day 1914.

2ND SCOTS GUARDS behind the lines, taking time out to play football, near Bac St Maur, November 1914. That year, Burnley had beaten Liverpool in the FA Cup Final.

“ THE OFFICERS GAVE THE ORDER, 'No fraternization', and then they turned their backs on us. But they didn't try to stop it because they knew they couldn't. We never said a word about the war to the Germans. We spoke about our families, about how old we were, how long we thought it would last and things like that. ”

Private Frank Sumpter, London Rifle Brigade

GERMAN SOLDIERS sleeping in their trench in the snow, prior to the Christmas truce, as two stand guard with rifles poised, near the Aisne River Valley, Western Front, France.

Opposite
BRITISH AND GERMAN SOLDIERS fraternizing at Ploegsteert, Belgium, on Christmas Day 1914. The Generals of both sides would ensure this never happened again.

WOUNDED BRITISH SOLDIER waiting for the Red Cross and
a train home to Blighty in time for the first Christmas of the war.
This was not the "It'll be over by Christmas" war that many had
anticipated when it began.

THE FUNERAL OF A PRIVATE of the 2nd Scots Guards – the body
is taken to the cemetery at Estaires, December 1914.

1915

- THE DERBY SCHEME

- BATTLE OF NEUVE CHAPELLE

- 2ND BATTLE OF YPRES AND FIRST USE OF GAS

- BATTLE OF AUBERS RIDGE

- BATTLE OF LOOS

- THE GALLIPOLI OFFENSIVE

THE SIDE OF A BUILDING IN *Fleet Street, London, is dedicated to the recruitment of young men, "For the defence of home and country", asking them to prove their courage and enlist. Two spy holes have the words "Can you look through? Yes! Then you are big enough and surely brave enough to serve your country" written next to them.*

combined with the yawning gulf in professional ability, enabled the Germans to drive the Russians out of Poland (a Russian province since the Napoleonic Wars) and, eventually, to overrun Serbia. Russian pressure on the tottering Austro-Hungarian Army was reduced, but this conquest of a great swathe of Eastern Europe availed Germany little. Russia remained in the war and the British and French war economies began to win the "battle of the factories".

The initial flood of British volunteers had, at first, stretched the ability of the tiny pre-war army to train and equip them, let alone command them in battle. Veteran officers and NCOs were brought from retirement, but the heavy losses that the pre-war regulars suffered in 1914 were to blunt the efficiency of this brave, enthusiastic but essentially amateur army. As 1915 wore on, volunteer numbers began to fall and nearly half of those coming forward were unsuitable on grounds of health. To bolster the numbers, "The Derby Scheme" was introduced. Under this scheme, men "attested to serve" on the understanding that they would only be called upon when necessary. Married men were assured that they would only be taken when all available single men had been called upon. Meanwhile, pressure to enlist was brought to bear in other ways: men out of uniform were handed white feathers, badges of cowardice, by women in the streets and Marie Lloyd, queen of the Music Halls, sang, "I didn't like you much before you joined the army, John, but I do like you, cockie, now you've got yer khaki on." and "We don't want to lose you, but we think you ought to go".

FRANCE HAD LOST TEN PER CENT OF HER TERRITORY to the German invasion, and a third of her industrial capacity. Nevertheless, French factories poured forth guns and munitions. At the same time, British industry was also attempting to make the transition to large-scale munitions production (see *above*) but levels of productivity often fell short of predictions, and standards of manufacture were alarmingly variable. A disagreeably high volume of "dud" shells were being passed to the front, leading to the so-called "Shell Crisis", which contributed to the downfall of the Liberal government and the establishment of a coalition in its place. The new government reorganized the national economy to boost military production and created a Ministry of Munitions under the leadership of David Lloyd George.

On the Western Front, a total of 110 Allied divisions were facing 100 German divisions. In the East, 80 German and Austro-Hungarian divisions were confronting 83 Russian divisions over a front that stretched from the Baltic Sea to the Carpathian Mountains – more than twice the length of the Western Front. The lower ratio of troops to space,

Early in 1915, the French kept steady pressure on the German lines while the BEF increased its strength. These assaults had chiefly been in the Artois region to the north and Champagne district to the south,

" *Marie Lloyd, queen of the music hall sang: 'I didn't like you much before you joined the army, John, but I do like you cockie, now you've got your khaki on.'* "

with the objective of crushing the German salient between Reims and Arras – and French casualties had been very high. The BEF was in no position to assist in any of these offensives, so the Battle of Neuve Chapelle was the first major test for the expanded BEF. The degree of success achieved indicated that, with a well-prepared artillery fireplan, it was possible to storm the German trenches. The village of Neuve Chapelle itself was not particularly significant, but just behind it lay Aubers Ridge, a piece of high ground that dominated the area. Sir Douglas Haig's First Army was to make the attack, in a two-pronged assault against the northern and southern sections of the German line, supported by a bombardment from six batteries of heavy 6-inch howitzers. More shells were discharged during this thirty-five minute bombardment than had been fired in the Boer War. The first stage of the attack on the morning of 10 March went well. Within two hours, five of the infantry battalions had claimed their objectives. Unfortunately the commanders didn't hammer home their advantage and the Germans were able to bring in reinforcements and more supplies, so enabling them to dig in and stop the British advance. By the time the attack was halted, both the British and the Germans had suffered around 11,000 casualties. The British had advanced a little over a mile. Compared with subsequent attacks, Neuve Chapelle was a small-scale operation, limited both in the numbers of troops employed and the modesty of the objectives.

The story of 1915 is one of progressively larger Allied assaults and ever-lengthening casualty lists. The Germans tried one brief attack in the West that year. On 22 April they made the first effective use of poison gas to attack French and British positions at Ypres. They then overran the positions affected by the gas with ease, as the French colonial and territorial troops took flight in terror. Yet the Germans failed to press home their advantage. The attack had essentially been an experimental raid, with no follow-up troops in position to exploit the gaps, which were plugged by a small force of British and Canadian troops. This mistake was to be repeated later by Allied forces.

At this stage, the only protection used against gas inhalation was to soak a cloth with urine and to place it against the nose and mouth. Thus equipped, the Allied armies faced up to a further gas attack two days later. The Allies condemned the use of gas as an atrocity – whilst hastily producing their own chemical weapons. It was the start of a chemical arms race which continued throughout the rest of the war.

Wanting to avoid further gas casualties, the Commander of the Second Army, Sir Horace Smith-Dorrien proposed a small withdrawal towards Ypres – which Sir John French rejected. Smith-Dorrien was promptly replaced by Herbert Plumer.

The French opened a major offensive in Artois, on a twenty-mile front from Vimy Ridge to Arras, on 9 May. Twenty French divisions were involved against just four German, but despite unprecedented artillery bombardments, the German defences proved impossible to break. Barbed wire obstructed the attackers' path, concealed machine guns swept the open approaches, and hidden batteries opened fire to cut the French to pieces in no-man's land.

Timed to coincide with this French attack, the BEF launched an attack on 9 May to take Aubers Ridge – but they had less artillery at their disposal than at Neuve Chapelle – and the Germans had increased their strength. The attack was a costly disaster, as only three of the twelve attacking battalions managed to reach the German front line. Eleven thousand lives had been lost by the time Haig called off the attack a day later.

Haig relaunched the Aubers Ridge attack five days later, but abandoned the former hurricane artillery bombardment for a more measured, methodical and carefully targeted bombardment, with more limited infantry objectives – but still casualty figures soared, and all for very little gain. The French tried again in the autumn on an even greater scale, this time with major British participation. Eighteen French divisions were ordered to assault the German lines in the Champagne sector, supported by 700 guns. Objectives up to fifty miles behind the German trenches were planned to be captured, but the lines barely advanced five miles.

Another thrust in the Artois area involved eleven French and five British divisions: the Battle of Loos opened on 25 September and ended on 8 October. The attack on Loos was the British contribution to the northern element of the autumn offensive; the French attacked Vimy Ridge, near Arras. The British deployed six divisions (seventy-five thousand men) on a wide front, with six divisions in reserve seven miles from the front. There was a four-day barrage, with a final four hours that exceeded in intensity any yet seen. Smoke barrages hid the advancing troops, and chlorine gas was used by the British for the first time. The Royal Flying Corps provided artillery reconnaissance and bombed communications targets. Loos was a coal-mining area before the war, and much of the fighting was for occupation of spoil heaps, such as Fosse 8, or their fortifications, such as the Hohenzollern Redoubt.

The attack began at 7.05 a.m. In the south, the village of Loos was taken by 8.00, and troops advanced to Hill 70, where they saw retreating Germans; but in following them, they were caught by fire from the prepared second line, and their advance was stopped by 10.30. In the north, the Hulloch Quarries were taken by 9.30; but casualties approached 70 per cent and the surviving troops halted until reserves could be brought up. The German observation posts were at the Hohenzollern Redoubt and Fosse 8, on the British left. After fierce fighting, particularly from the Cameron Highlanders, and accurate artillery fire, the Quarries and both posts were in British hands by midnight.

The Germans counter-attacked at about 1.00, taking the Quarries but failing at Fosse 8; the British attack was renewed at 9.00, with an assault on Hill 70, which failed. These positions were attacked and counter-attacked many times, with gas attacks by both sides, until 13 October, when the failure of the French 10th Army to draw off German reserves, severe casualties and bad weather brought the offensive to an end with Loos village in British hands.

The German lines had remained unbroken, despite the British use of gas and smoke. Heavy British casualties helped to end the career of the British Expeditionary Force commander, Sir John French. He was replaced by the commander of the First Army, General Haig. On the French side, Joffre's reputation suffered, but he retained his position.

With such heavy casualties and so little movement on the Western Front, the British had been looking further afield in their attempt to achieve a breakthrough. Their plan had been to create a major diversion by knocking the southernmost of the Central Powers, Turkey, out of the war. This would serve a dual purpose, undermining the German campaign and opening up the area of the Dardanelles for supplies into Russia. The Ottoman Empire had joined Germany and Austro-Hungary in October 1914, and the First Lord of the Admiralty, Winston Churchill, saw this as an opportunity to inflict the necessary damage with an almost entirely naval force and only limited support by ground troops, but Kitchener eventually diverted the Australian Imperial Force and a substantial number of New Zealanders en route to the Western Front to form a new ANZAC army. The specific aim was to secure the peninsula, clear it of Turkish defences and thus allow a British fleet to enter the Sea of Marmara. General Sir Ian Hamilton was given command of the Constantinople

" One final attempt was made to break the Turkish lines in August, resulting only in more loss of life. "

Expeditionary Force, of seventy-five thousand men, but the well-prepared Turkish Fifth Army, under the command of the German Liman von Sanders, had eighty-four thousand men distributed in six divisions across the peninsula.

The Allied naval attack at the Dardanelles on 19 March 1915 was beaten off – and three battleships were lost. The decision was then taken to land the ANZAC force, along with a French Expeditionary Force on the Gallipoli peninsula whose task would be to clear the way in for the Navy. These landings took place on 25 April, the Australian troops going ashore to the north at Anzac Cove, while British and French troops landed at Cape Helles. Almost immediately the troops were bogged down, with the 29th Division sustaining particularly heavy losses at Lancashire Landing, where six Victoria Crosses were awarded to men of one battalion for the actions of that one morning. The Allies spent the rest of the year in trench warfare, with losses heavy on both sides as successive attacks were repelled. One final attempt was made to break the Turkish lines in August, resulting in more loss of life. General Munro recommended that the Allies pull out of the peninsula – and eventually the troop evacuation was started under the cover of darkness on the night of 15 December, with the rest of the forces following on 8 January. More than 250,000 men had become casualties or been taken prisoner, and as a result, Lord Kitchener's reputation suffered a major blow. Winston Churchill had already been replaced as First Lord of the Admiralty, after the failure of the naval attack. 1915 proved to be a wasteful and inconclusive year for the British. The High Command was aware that rigorous recruitment would need to be undertaken to keep the lines manned.

Below
Troops depart Gallipoli.

GERMAN TROOPS, obviously some way from the front, celebrating New Year's Eve.

A RECRUITING SERGEANT of the RAMC attempts to enlist
recruits the old-fashioned way, eye-balling his would-be soldiers,
and telling them of the noble future that awaits them.

Opposite
NEW RECRUITS – of various shapes, sizes and ages, line up
for inspection in Bermondsey, London.

" WHEN THEY CAME TO US they were weedy, sallow, skinny, frightened children
– the refuse of our industrial system – and they were in very poor condition because
of wartime food shortages. But after six months of good food, fresh air and physical
exercise they changed so much their mothers wouldn't have recognized them. "

Lieutenant Charles Carrington, 1/5th Battalion Warwickshire Regiment

MEN OF THE QUEEN Victoria Rifles, 9th London Regiment,
seen during training in Hampstead, in January 1915.

Opposite
MEN OF THE LONDON SCOTTISH, 2nd Battalion at
a training camp in Saffron Walden, Essex.

" I'VE **OFTEN THOUGHT HOW** our training didn't relate to what we had to face; the company drill, physical training, route marches, gymnastics and such things. Why go to all that trouble, when in the end, you only had to look after yourself? "

Corporal John Oborne, 4th Battalion Devonshire Regiment

COMPANY OFFICERS of the 13th (Service) Wandsworth Battalion of
the East Surrey Regiment, saluting Captain F.A.M. Webster, at Thames
Ditton, 7 February 1915.

Opposite
DRUMMER DRISCOLE of 3/20th London Regiment,
seen in football kit at training camp.

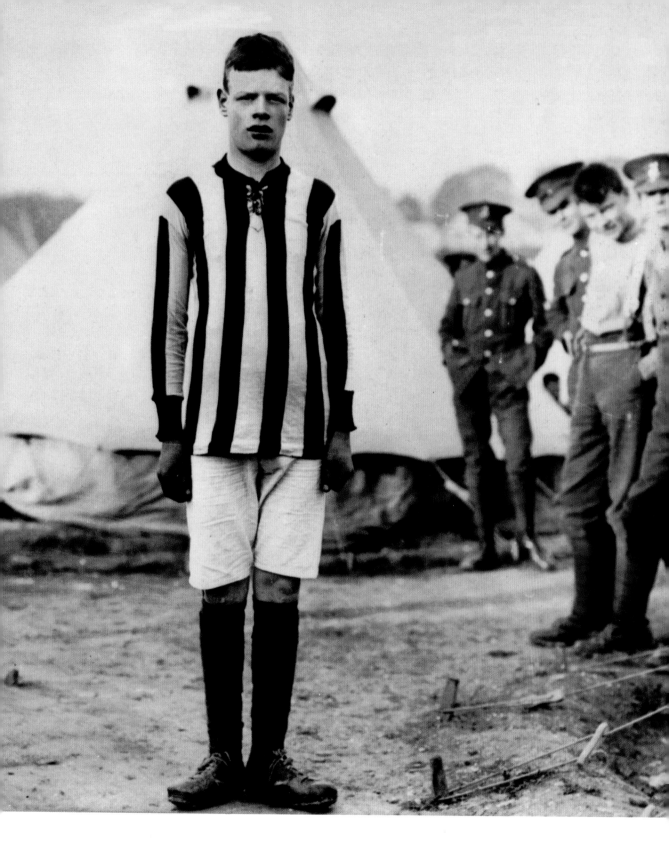

MEN OF THE SOUTH STAFFORDSHIRE
Regiment with a Belgian baby and some new friends.

" WE SQUATTED DOWN, and I saw that one of the young women was nursing a baby. For something to say, I said 'Is your baby alright?'. With a sad smile she said, 'It is not my baby. I don't even know her mother.' My pal and I emptied from our haversacks two tins of sardines and army biscuits. 'The baby needs milk,' she said. I remembered I'd earlier filled my water bottle with milk from a deserted farm. 'Give her some of this, 'I said. I think even the baby was surprised. "

Sergeant Richard Tobin, Hood Battalion, Royal Naval Division

" OUR LIVING CONDITIONS were lousy, dirty and insanitary – no matter what the weather was, whether it was hot or cold, rain or fine, you were in there for four days and three nights. There were rats as big as cats and if you had any leather equipment the damn things would gnaw at it. For four months I was in France I never had a bath, and I never had any clean clothes to put on. "

Harry Patch, Cornwall Light Infantry

GORDON HIGHLANDERS AT LAVENTIE, March 1915 having a quick wash
(*opposite*). Two soldiers use the water collected in a shell-hole to wash and shave (*above*).

Overleaf
2ND BATTALION ARGYLL AND SUTHERLAND Highlanders, in their
government-issue fur jackets.

THE SECOND BATTLE OF YPRES. Men of the Honorable Artillery Company in front-line trench at St Eloi, opposite the Mound, April 1915, with one using a box periscope.

Opposite
THE GERMANS enjoyed far superior trench construction systems than the Allies, both in terms of protection from the conditions, and from enemy shell-fire.

" ON A NICE SUMMER'S DAY you could think there wasn't a war on, really. Looking through the periscope out to no-man's-land you would see the sandbags of the Germans' front line, you would see the grass and the flowers out front – the birds might start singing if the sun was up on a nice day... But it did happened sometimes – people would forget and get careless, and before you knew where you were they had got a bullet through their head while sitting on the latrine or something. "

Private Ernest Todd

THE BATTLE OF AUBERS Ridge
(Fromelles), 9 May 1915, showing
the men of 'C' Company, 2nd Lincolnshire
Regiment, inside a mine crater.

Opposite
FRENCH SOLDIERS REMOVE corpses
from a trench after fighting at Bagatelle in
the Argonne. During the Second Battle of
Ypres, the Allies lost 69,000 men.

" UNTIL THE DEAD ARE BURIED they change somewhat
in appearance each day. The colour change in Caucasian
races is from white to yellow, to yellow-green, to black.
If left long enough in the heat the flesh comes to resemble
coal-tar, especially where it has been broken or torn, and
it has quite a visible tarlike iridescence. The dead grow
larger each day until sometimes they become quite
too big for their uniforms, filling these until they seem
blown tight enough to burst. The individual members
may increase in girth to an unbelievable extent and
faces fill as taut and globular as balloons. "

Ernest Hemingway, A Natural History of the Dead

Above and opposite

'Y' WOOD, HOOGE, AT 6 AM, 16 June, 1915. The flag on the right was put up to show that a German trench had been captured, and that the troops were going on. Men of the King's Regiment (Liverpool Scottish) are taking cover under the parapet of the captured German front line. The officer standing with the cap on is the Forward Observation Officer.

" I HAD A SENSE that there was definitely something wrong – that something was brewing. I was determined that everyone should be up and alert and should have their bayonet fixed because I hated the feeling that something wasn't right. I was at the farthest point away from the crater when the thing happened... The first idea that flitted through my mind was that the end of the world had come, and this was the Day of Judgement, because the whole dawn had turned a ghastly crimson-red. As I began to come to my senses, I saw four or five jets of flame passing across the trench that I had been in just one minute before. There was a horrible hissing sound and a nasty oily black smoke at the edge of the flame. They were using flame-throwers. "

Lieutenant Gordon Carey

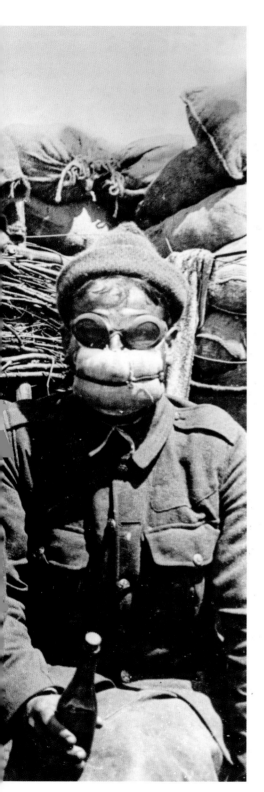

2ND BATTALION ARGYLL AND SUTHERLAND HIGHLANDERS, Bois Grenier Sector, 1915. With the wide-spread use of gas as a weapon by this time, basic respirators were hurriedly brought into use for front line troops.

TROOPS ADVANCING to the attack through gas – a remarkable private photograph taken by a member of the London Rifle Brigade on the opening day of the Battle of Loos, 25 September 1915.

" AFTER THE GAS ATTACK the men came tumbling from the front line. I have never before seen men so terror stricken, they were tearing at their throats and their eyes were glaring out. **"**

Private W.A. Quinton 2nd Battalion, Bedfordshire Regiment

BRITISH TROOPS RETURNING
from the line after the Battle of Loos,
September-October 1915.

❝ WHEN THEY TOOK THE ROLL CALL after Loos those
not answering, their chums would answer: 'Over the Hill'.
Also when the post and parcels that had arrived from
Home were being dished out after Loos, we new arrivals
got share of the parcels that were meant for the boys
who got killed. ❞

Private Carson Stewart

A FIRING SQUAD composed of British soldiers, take aim at a German spy. But it was not always the enemy who faced summary execution.

ON THE NIGHT of 13/14 October 1915, Zeppelins accounted for the lives of 71 Londoners and many were wounded including these two children.

" ONE MINUTE, I'M IN THE STREET and the next I'm in bed. I didn't know where I was and I didn't know what had happened. I was told that a 'Zeppelin' had dropped a bomb, but that meant nothing to me. "

Child in London

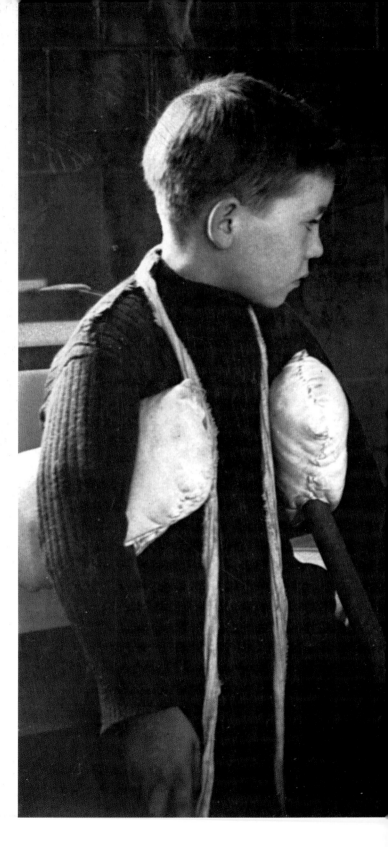

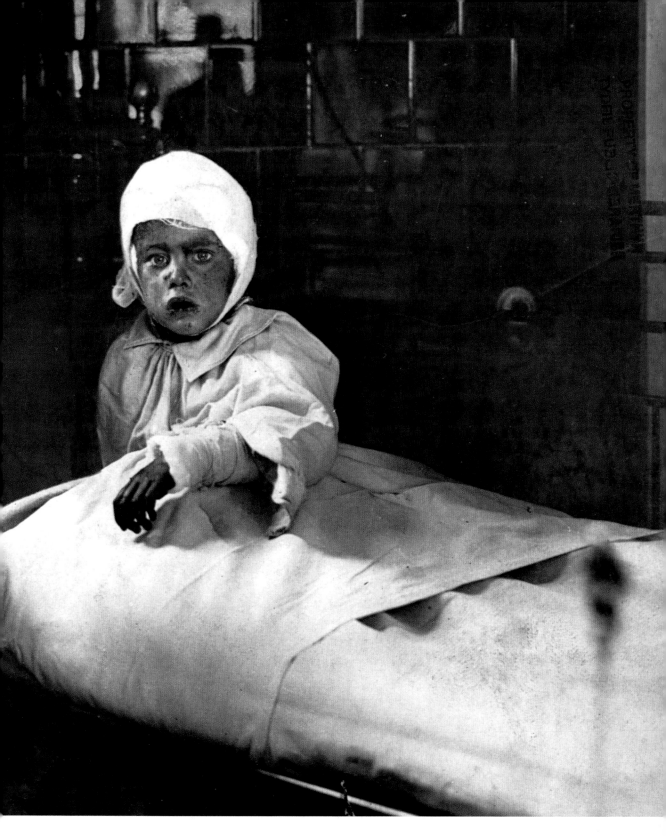

1915 [105]

AUSTRALIANS LANDING AT GALLIPOLI, in a bay later named ANZAC Cove at 8 am, 25 April 1915. These men are part of the Australian 4th Battalion (1st Brigade). At the water's edge is the body of Sapper R. Reynolds, one of the first men to be killed at Gallipoli.

Opposite
GALLIPOLI – Royal Marines landing on 25 April 1915.

❝ WE HAD TO RUN down the gangway across the two boats and a steam hopper, and then we only had perhaps ten or twenty feet to go to the shore. But the boat had been carried away towards a strip of rock, and the steam hopper and one of the lighters had been cut away and drifted out to sea. The one that was tied to the bow of the ship was all right, but as we ran down the gangway, instead of having two separate gangways either side of the ship, they had connected them. Unfortunately the first batch had to run across into the lighter, and what with us running down and them running across, and all the bodies piling up, it was like a barricade. They simply fell into the lighters. Some were dead, some were wounded. Some weren't hit but got smothered in the pile-up. **❞**

Fusilier W. Flynn, 1st Royal Munster Fusiliers

THE DEFENCE OF ANZAC COVE. Scene in a trench during the period 28 April-12 May, when the Marine and 1st Naval Brigades of the Royal Naval Division reinforced the Australian and New Zealand Army Corps in the area about what were later known as "Quinn's" and "Courtney's" Posts. The Marines brought a few periscopes with them, and the Australians improvised a supply from looking-glasses sent ashore from transports.

Opposite
HELLES, 4 JUNE. Men of the King's own Scottish Borderers go over the top.

❝ WE STOOD THERE, packed like sardines, unable to stand up in comfort, and we still had another hour to go before we went over the top. It was a long hour. Some men were fast asleep on their feet, others just stood staring at the sky. The laddie next to me checked his rifle and ammunition again and again, still not satisfied. Others just stood and stared, silent as the grave. ❞

Ordinary Seaman Joe Murray, Hood Battalion, Royal Naval Division

A TURKISH SNIPER photographed immediately after capture, and while he was being brought in under guard. The Turk was ingeniously screened by a Jack-in-the-Green arrangement of foliage attached to his clothing.

Opposite
THE IRREPRESSIBLE AUSTRALIANS at ANZAC Cove. An Australian bringing in a wounded comrade to hospital. The men were cracking jokes as they made their way down from the front.

1916

- CAPTURE OF ST. ELOI
- BATTLE OF VERDUN
- BATTLE OF THE SOMME
- BATTLE OF MORVAL
- BATTLE OF THIEPVAL RIDGE
- BATTLE OF THE ANCRE

WOUNDED GERMAN PRISONER OF WAR *being treated for a head injury by an English soldier.*

At the start of 1916, the British war cabinet accepted that volunteers alone could no longer make up for the losses sustained on the Western Front, and on 27 January, conscription was introduced in the form of the Military Service Act. The new recruits, however, were not up to the standard of the seasoned, career-trained men who had been lost – and the German Army set about capitalising on earlier losses and the inexperience of the fresh troops. With massively increased firepower on both sides and large numbers of new men brought into the trenches, the scale of operations was increased, and with it the level of violence and devastation – and the number of casualties that the year would bring.

The German strategy in 1916 was to force the Allies to defend at points of their choosing. The objective was not to win ground but to cause unsustainable casualties; Verdun, which was fought from February to December, was expressed as an attempt "to bleed the French Army white".

General Falkenhayn's strategy was to deliver the heaviest blow he could against France, perhaps calculating that after the hideous losses of 1914–15

the French might conceivably crack. The blow was to be aimed at Verdun, close to Metz, which had been occupied by Germany since 1871, and had served as a major depot for their armies ever since. For an attack in this sector the German railway network could ferry hundreds of heavy guns right up to the front line, together with vast quantities of ammunition.

More than a thousand guns and mortars fired two million rounds at the French front line to open the battle, but despite this, the first infantry attacks mounted on 21 February met with heroic resistance. Further bombardments were launched, after which the Germans ground their way forward, very slowly. Their rate of advance was little more than half a mile a day during the first week, and they came to a virtual halt in March.

As the Battle of Verdun proceeded, the French urged the British to stage an offensive to relieve the pressure on their forces. The resulting British attack was mounted on The Somme. The Germans had fortified their positions on The Somme with professional thoroughness. Three successive lines of defences followed the high ground across gently undulating farmland. The Germans held a line along a low chalk ridge, whose position was substantially unchanged from that taken in 1914: it was, however, very much more formidably defended, with two trench systems, each with several lines and connected by communications trenches, thick belts of barbed wire "so dense that daylight could barely be seen through it", according to one British machine-gunner, and deep concrete dugouts. Machine-guns in concrete strong-points were deployed with interlocking zones of fire, most sited to fire into the flank of attacking infantry. The chalky soil was excellent for tunneling, and German engineers burrowed deep to create almost indestructible

❝ As the Battle of Verdun proceeded, the French urged the British to stage an offensive to relieve the pressure on their forces. ❞

shelters for the soldiers manning the front line. German artillery positions lay well back, camouflaged from the air but ready to pour fire into no-man's-land, directed by observation positions whose telephone lines were buried deep under the shell-torn ground.

The British plan was not unlike General Falkenhayn's at Verdun: to pulverise the enemy trenches with such a weight of fire that the trenches would collapse, the barbed wire would be cut and resistance could be brushed aside. Again like the Germans at Verdun, it was anticipated that the greatest danger would be from enemy counter-attacks catching the assault troops unawares after their initial success. Consequently, leading waves carried picks, shovels and sandbags with which to fortify their positions once they had captured them. No British artilleryman had ever had so much firepower at his disposal.

The objectives of the Somme offensive were strategic, not tactical: according to Sir William Robertson, Chief of the Imperial General Staff, "The necessity of relieving pressure on the French Army at Verdun remains, and is more urgent than ever. This is, therefore, the first objective to be obtained by the combined British and French offensive. The second objective is to inflict as heavy losses as possible upon the German armies."

The Somme was in part chosen because it was where the British and French lines joined, and the French would make a smaller attack to the south. The part of the line chosen for the French attack ran from just north of Lihons to Curlu on the river (about nine miles), and then to Maricourt (three thousand yards). The British sector ran from there north-west to Fricourt, then to the River Ancre, then north in front of Beaumont-Hamel and Serre. The total British frontage was more than 25 miles; the French, 11. A subsidiary attack was to be made at the German salient at Gommecourt, further north.

The bombardment lasted a week, beginning on 24 June. Five days of intensive shelling was planned,

with pauses to trick the Germans into manning their front line trenches and unmasking their hidden batteries. This was extended by two days as the attack, intended for 29 June, had to be delayed until 1 July because of bad weather. Zero hour was fixed after first light at the request of the French, who wanted good observation for their artillery; many British officers had wanted to go over the top while it was still dark. At 7.20 a.m. on 1 July Hawthorn Mine was detonated under a strong-point protecting the village of Beaumont-Hamel. Despite leaving a crater forty feet deep and three hundred feet wide, the Germans held on, and Beaumont-Hamel was not finally taken until 13 November. The barrage lifted at 7.30 a.m, and sixteen more mines were detonated.

The whistles blew at 7.30 am and tens of thousands of men clambered up the assault ladders and into no-man's-land. They advanced at a walking pace so as not to become disorganised. It was not long before they realised that the bombardment had failed to crush the enemy defences; along most of the line the dugouts had not been destroyed and the wire was intact. Much of the British artillery on the Somme consisted of field guns firing shrapnel and these guns had made little impact on the wire. Nor were the German machine-guns destroyed or even suppressed. The machine-gunners continued to occupy their strong-points, and across the twenty-mile front, British hopes were dashed by the steady stutter of the Maxim guns. The German artillery counter-barrage opened with murderous effect, deluging no-man's-land with high explosive and in some sectors wrecking the British front-line trenches. On that day of unimaginable horror, the British Army suffered 57,470 casualties, 19,240 of them fatal. It remains the army's greatest loss on a single day.

Two weeks after the initial attack, Haig ordered an attack on the second line, which took place at 3.25 a.m. on 14 July. Three days later, the British line was established from Maltz Horn Farm to the north of Ovillers. High Wood, a crucial position at the top of the ridge, was not held. Despite the cavalry finally coming into action and clearing it on the 14th, it was counter-attacked. The flanks could not advance to support it, and the troops were pulled back on the 15th. This left Delville Wood and Longueval, which had been taken at great cost by the South African Brigade, as a vulnerable salient. To the left Pozières and Thiepval and to the right Guillemont remained in German hands. The forward troops in the salient were therefore vulnerable to concentrated fire, and the immediate objective was to prevent the salient being driven in. Haig paused to relieve his front line troops, move guns forward and improve his communications and on 18 July, the Germans made their expected counter-attack on the salient.

This phase of the battle saw a succession of small advances and fierce counter-attacks, with the key positions changing hands many times. By the end of August there were five times as many German divisions on the British front as there had been on 1 July, but they were believed to be exhausted and short of ammunition. Accordingly, at noon on 3 September an assault was launched from the Ancre in the north to the extreme right of the line, supported by the French in their sector. Six days later, Beaumont-Hamel and Thiepval remained in German hands, as did the ground initially captured between High Wood and Delville Wood, but Guillemont and Ginchy had fallen, the second line penetrated, and about five miles of the nearer crest of the ridge held.

Haig paused a further week, waiting for reinforcements, and it was on 15 September that the British attacked on a ten-mile front between Combles and the Ancre valley beyond Thiepval. Twelve divisions took part, their attack supported by thirty-six armoured fighting vehicles – "tanks" – which were used for the first time. Key objectives were the village of Courcelette, just west of the road; and east of the road High Wood, Flers, Lesboeufs and Morval. On the left Courcelette was captured by the Canadians and the ridge in the centre was held, but on the right the Guards and 6th Divisions failed to reach Lesboeufs and Morval.

Morval was attacked again on the 25th, and taken, and the next day the village of Guedecourt fell. Thiepval was finally taken, with a thousand prisoners, on the morning of the 27th. By the beginning of October, Haig was in a position to push the centre forward, turn the positions on the Ancre, and secure the ridge. On the right, the Le Transloy line was smashed and the German position from the Ancre to Morval was taken. This had been the original objective on 1 July. Subsequently, however, the weather changed and October and early November were very wet. In Haig's words: "The country roads, broken by countless shell craters, that crossed the deep stretch of ground we had lately won, rapidly became almost impassable, making the supply of food, stores and ammunition a serious problem. These conditions multiplied the difficulties of attack to such an extent that it was found impossible to exploit the situation with the rapidity necessary to enable us to reap the full benefits of the advantages we had gained." In the words of the Official History, the battlefield was by then "a wilderness of mud", where "holding water-logged trenches or shell-hole posts, accessible only by night, the infantry abode in conditions which might be likened to those of earth-worms, rather than of human-kind".

By 13 November the weather had cleared, and Haig attacked on both sides of the Ancre. The 63rd (RN) Division took and held Beaucourt, and the 51st (Highland) finally captured Beaumont-Hamel. The

> *" The casualty lists published in Britain staggered the nation. "*

last attack before foul weather precluded further offensives was on the high ground between Grandcourt and Pys. In four and a half months the Allied lines had advanced an average of five miles on the fourteen-mile front, two-thirds in the British sector. Casualties were 419,654 British, 204,253 French and 465,000–680,000 German.

The casualty lists published in Britain staggered the nation, especially as the territorial gains were so negligible. Yet the battle was an equally grim experience for the Germans. The unbending Prussian tradition of "Halten, was zu halten ist" ("Hold on to whatever can be held") was applied with no regard for the lives of the soldiers. On almost any given day of the Somme battle the Germans launched some sort of counter-attack, in the teeth of massive British fire superiority. If the British gunners failed to wipe out the German infantry in the pre-battle bombardment, they made up for it with deadly

accurate fire that smashed many a German counter-blow even as it assembled on its start line. The Royal Artillery fired seven million rounds on The Somme between 2 July and 15 September, and by the end of the battle 138 German divisions had been rotated in and out of the front line there, compared with seventy-five at Verdun.

WOUNDED SOLDIERS playing football outside Blenheim Palace, Oxfordshire, 1916.
Not only British, but also Allied soldiers were sent to England to recuperate, before being
sent home or back to the front.

SOLDIERS CONVALESCING from their injuries salute the changing of the guard at Buckingham Palace, London, 1916.

YOUNG WORKERS in Swan Hunter and Wigham Richardson's ship-building yard, Newcastle. Ship-building was one of the reserved occupations, considered important enough to the country that those serving in them were exempt from military service.

Opposite
BRITISH SOLDIERS saying goodbye to their families at Victoria Station as they embark for the continent, 1916.

" THAT NIGHT I WAS terribly upset. I told him I didn't want him to go and be a soldier – I didn't want to lose him. I didn't want him to go at all. But he said, 'We have to go. There has to be men to go.' **"**

Kitty Eckersly, mill-worker ·

THREE GERMAN SOLDIERS display rats killed in their trench the previous night. Rats showed no allegiance. They plagued the German and British trenches alike.

" **EVEN THE RATS** used to become hysterial. They came into our flimsy shelters to seek refuge from the terrific artillery fire. "

Lieutenant Stefan Westmann, German army

Opposite

GERMAN SOLDIERS tackle the ever-present problem of lice. In the absence of a candle, the only way to deal with them was to catch them individually and crush them between the fingernails. The British troops were similarly infested.

A FRENCH SOLDIER talks to German troops across the sandbags of their trench.

Opposite

BRITISH TROOPS resting in their trench – note the private has taken off the troublesome puttees that most of the soldiers detested putting on.

" **IT IS A COMMENTARY** on modern war that commanders should fear lest the soldiers on each side become friendly. Our soldiers have no quarrel with 'Fritz', save during the heat of battle, or in retaliation for some blow below the belt. If whole armies fraternized, politicians on both sides would be sore set to solve their problems. Yet it is possible that if there had been a truce for a fortnight on the whole trench-line at any time after the battle of the Somme, the war might have ended – and what would mother have said then? "

Colonel W.N. Nicholson, Staff Officer, Suffolk Regiment

A GROUP OF GERMAN SOLDIERS going through a de-lousing ritual.

Opposite
MEN STANDING on a firestep looking over into no-man's land.

❝ I THINK THE WORST THING of the whole war was being so lousy. You had a candle and you got in this little dugout – just a hole in a trench – and you lit the candle. You took your shirt off and you'd run the seams along the flame of the candle and it would kill all the eggs. You could do that today, but you'd be just as bad tomorrow. ❞

Albert "Smiler" Marshall, 1st Battalion Essex Yeomanry

MEN OF THE 4TH BATTALION, Suffolk Regiment keeping an anxious eye on the German trenches.

" STANDING ON THE FRONT LINE of a firing step was very uncomfortable, with nothing to do and not much to talk about. I think it made you consider life much more deeply than one would have done otherwise. *"*

Corporal Sidney Amatt, London Rifle Brigade

WALTER TULL, professional footballer and the first black officer in the British Army:-

Walter was born *in Folkestone in 1888. By the age of nine he had lost both his parents and he was sent to an orphanage in Bethnal Green. In 1909, he signed for Tottenham Hotspur as a professional – the second black professional footballer in Britain. When war broke out, he joined the 17th (1st Football) Battalion of the Middlesex Regiment. In November 1915 he was sent to France and Tull was promoted to Sergeant. In July, he took part in the Somme offensive. In 1917, despite military regulations forbidding "any negro or person of colour" being made an officer, he received a commission. On March 25, 1918, 2nd Lieutenant Tull was killed during an attack on German trenches at Favrueil. His body was never recovered.*

FOOT INSPECTION by the Medical Officer of the 12th East Yorkshires in a support trench. The steel helmet was first worn in March 1916.

NORTHUMBERLAND FUSILIERS wearing German helmets
and gas masks captured at St. Eloi, 27 March, 1916.

GERMAN PRISONERS captured by the Northumberland
Fusiliers and the Royal Fusiliers in the attack on St. Eloi.

A GERMAN INFANTRYMAN during the battle at Verdun, oblivious to the rotting French soldier beside him.

❝ FOR A YOUNG MAN who had a long and worthwhile future awaiting him, it was not easy to expect death almost daily. However, after a while I got used to the idea of dying young. Strangely, it had a sort of soothing effect, and prevented me from worrying too much. Because of this I gradually lost the terrible fear of being wounded or killed. ❞

Reinhold Spengler, German volunteer

FRENCH TROOPS use large stones and rocks to dislodge German soldiers from hillside trenches during the battle of Verdun.

THE SCENE IN a communication trench in the build-up to the
battle of Albert, July 1916.

GAS SENTRY ringing the gas alarm near Fleurbaix. Various warning bells and rattles were used. The sentry is wearing a helmet which was impregnated with hyposulphate of soda and phenate to protect him.

THE BARRAGE WHICH PRECEDED the battle of the Somme
began on 24 June. In the week that followed, 1,732,873 shells were
fired by British guns along the 14 mile Front. At its height, on the
morning of 1 July, the barrage could be heard on Hampstead Heath
in north London.

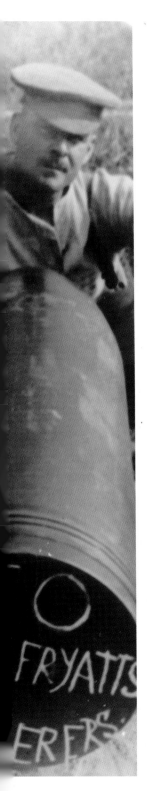

GERMAN INFANTRY in a shelter wait anxiously for the British bombardment to end.

Opposite

MEN OF THE ROYAL MARINE ARTILLERY with 15-inch shells. These were the heaviest shells used by Royal Marine Gunners on the Somme. The chalk lettering: "To Captain Fryatt's murderers" is a reference to the execution of Captain Charles Fryatt, a British Merchant Navy officer. While in command of a Great Eastern Railway steamer, *Brussels*, Fryatt had attempted to ram a German submarine. Weeks later, the Germans boarded the *Brussels* and seized Fryatt. He was tried for piracy, found guilty and shot.

LAYING A CHARGE in a mine chamber, before the battle of Albert. The officer is using a geophone which detects sound and vibrations underground.

Opposite
BATTLE OF ALBERT – After the explosion of the mine at Beaumont Hamel, 1 July 1916.

"AT ABOUT 7AM, La Boisselle went up. It went up slowly and whole houses started splitting and falling apart in the air. Great elm trees were going up, their roots turning upside down. When they reached the top they disintegrated into bits and pieces and dust and clouds. it was an awesome sight. **"**

Fusilier Victor Packer

ZERO HOUR the whistles were blown. Ladders were put up to mount out of the trench and lanes had been cut through the 30 foot British wire. We had been told 'there's no need for this short rushes and getting down on your stomach, go straight over as if you were on parade. There's no fear of enemy attack! That's been silenced by the British guns!' **"**

Corporal James Tansley, 9th Battalion, Yorkshire and Lancashire Regiment

CANADIAN TROOPS prepare to go over the top at the Somme at the beginning of day one of the battle. They believed they would be mopping up survivors and leading the final breakthrough into French countryside!

Above

MEN OF THE 1ST BATTALION Lancashire Fusilers fix bayonets before going into the attack. They would encounter stiff German resistance. Many of these men would be dead before the hour was out.

BATTLE OF ALBERT – British troops attacking German trenches near Mametz. A shrapnel shell is bursting overhead.

Opposite
CREW OF A GERMAN MG 08 machine-gun, Western Front.

" WE WERE ATTACKING the last German trench. We were all knocked out.
Their machine guns were waiting for us. We didn't get through. None of us.
The whole battalion was wiped out. There was a big shell hole full of dead
men and dying and blinded. Tall men got it through the jaw, shorter men
through the eyes. I was walking along and a bullet blew all my teeth out. "

Segeant James Payne, 16th Battalion, Manchester Regiment

A BRITISH DRESSING STATION, after the battle.

Opposite
WOUNDED BRITISH MEN and German prisoners.

" EVERYTHING HAS GONE WELL. Our troops have successfully carried out their missions, all counter-attacks have been repulsed and large numbers of prisoners taken. "

The Times, reporting on 3 July 1916 on the disastrous Battle of the Somme

13TH ROYAL FUSILIERS celebrating with many souvenirs, with so much more action to come, this was a short respite.

“ ONE OF THE ENEMY SOLDIERS removed his water bottle and passed it to me. I will never forget this gesture as long as I live. ”

Gefreiter Fritz Heinemann, Somme

BATTLE OF THE SOMME, 1916. Men of the Wiltshire Regiment returning with German caps, helmets and prisoner, Bouzincourt, August 1916.

DERELICT hansom cab found in Bazentin-le-Grand.

ARTILLERY ON THE ROAD, Aveluy, September 1916. The backbone of any British attack was the vanguard of artillery bombardments. Here, as one unit retires, another moves up to the front.

Opposite
BATTLE OF MORVAL Supporting troops following the first line of attack, 25 September 1916.

   ❝ DURING A BATTLE you couldn't tell how many were killed on either side.
All you knew was what your part was. There could be a terrible battle going
on no further away than the end of your lane, but you wouldn't know until
you were told next morning that your mate was killed. You'd only know the
part of the battle that you could see, but the rest was just a matter of shells
bursting here, bursting there – bursting everywhere – and you couldn't get
out of the way of them. ❞

Albert 'Smiler' Marshall, Essex Yeomanry

THE BRITISH MILITARY CEMETERY "Windmill", at Monchy-le-Preux, with bodies laid out awaiting burial.

Opposite
THE PACKS BELONGING TO DEAD AND WOUNDED men lie waiting to be searched, south of Guillemont, September 1916. The letters and treasured items found will be sent home to the next of kin.

" DEATH! BEFORE THIS WAR, WE DID NOT DIE: we ended. Neatly, in the shelter of a room, in the warmth of a bed. Now, we die. It is the wet death, the muddy death, death dripping with blood. The bodies lie frozen in the earth which gradually sucks them in. The luckiest depart, wrapped in canvas, to sleep in the nearest cemetery. "

L. Mairet, killed in action, April 1917

AN EXHAUSTED BRITISH SOLDIER lost in thought, near Aveluy Wood, September 1916. The full horror of the casualties would not sink in for months to come.

MEN OF THE 1ST WILTSHIRE REGIMENT playing football near
Bouzincourt, September 1916.

Opposite
ONE OF THE BEST LUXURIES of being taken out of the front line
– the chance to bath, delouse – and get clean kit.

" LICE – I DIDN'T HAVE LICE. They had me. The seams of your trousers used to be their nesting place – you'd have to run the seams over a candle. I always remember, there was one chappie, as we were delousing, he used to say, 'Ah, little chap. I'm going to put you back – and have you tomorrow when you're bigger.' There was a comical side to it all, but it was dreary sometimes. It's pretty boring, war. "

John Oborne, Royal Horse Artillery

BATTLE OF GUINCHY. Carrying the wounded across the battlefield under shellfire, 9 September 1916.

Opposite
BRITISH TROOPS returning from trenches at Carney, September 1916.

" OUR BATTALION WAS MOVED BACK into the reserve trenches and another battalion took our place in the front line, ready to go over the top at dawn the next day. As they marched past us on their way to take up their positions, they were all lustily singing a sentimental song of the period, which was not only pathetic but also prophetic. It went thus: 'Break the news to Mother, tell her there is no other / Tell her not to wait for me for I'm not coming home.' "

Private A.L. Atkins, 1/7th Middlesex Regiment

MEN OF THE 5TH NORTHUMBERLAND FUSILIERS

waiting for haircuts, October 1916.

THREE WOUNDED, returning from Dernancourt, September 1916,
their humour still intact – one of them wears a German helmet.

THE RESULT OF devastating British artillery fire. (*Opposite*) Dead war horses are buried in a mass grave.

❝ THE WHOLE EARTH is ploughed by the exploding shells. Broken wagons and dead horses are moved to the sides of the road, also many dead soldiers lie here. Their eyes stare at you. Sometimes an arm or leg is missing. ❞

Hans Otto Schetter, German musketeer

" I WON'T SAY HORSES WON the war for us, but we would never have won it without them. "

Private Fred Lloyd, Royal Field Artillery

A WORKING PARTY in waterproofs and trench waders, carrying
shovels, about to start off in the rain near St Pierre Division, during
the last phase of the British Somme offensive, 10-11 November 1916.

Opposite
A BRITISH MILITARY policeman with a wounded German soldier,
St. Pierre Division 13 November 1916

A FRENCH SOLDIER stands amongst dead comrades.

❝ THE WEATHER WAS VERY HOT and I was sent up to an observation post. We found we literally couldn't walk along the trenches without treading on dead bodies. German and British. The stench and the flies were simply appalling. ❞

Lieutenant Montague Cleeve, Royal Garrison Artillery

GERMAN SOLDIERS removing their dead by the carload after the siege of Verdun. Both sides were bled dry of reinforcements. During the 10 month battle over a quarter of a million men of both sides lost their lives. No strategic or tactical advantage was gained by either side.

A VICTIM'S HAND on the battlefield of Verdun.

A TRAUMATIZED French soldier smokes his pipe in one of the forts of Verdun after the battle.

Overleaf
TOMMIES resting in a bombed out building.

❝ VERDUN. WHAT A BLOOD BATH, what horrid images, what slaughter. Hell cannot be this dreadful. ❞

Alfred Jombaire, last recorded words in his diary

A COFFEE STALL transported from London, at Auchonvillers, November 1916.

Opposite
RATHER OPTIMISTIC cavalrymen, with mistletoe in their caps, meeting their forthcoming Christmas dinner, Bailleul, December 1916.

❝ THE DAILY MAIL used to send two-pound tins of Christmas pudding for us at the front. They sent them every Christmas, and the officers would wait on the men for their Christmas dinner. Everyone had a portion of Christmas pudding from the tin. ❞

Cecil Withers, East Surrey Regiment

1917

- THE USA JOINS THE WAR
- THE TAKING OF VIMY RIDGE
- BATTLE OF ARRAS
- BATTLE OF PILCKEM RIDGE
- PASSCHENDAELE
- BATTLE OF CAMBRAI

THE RAVAGES OF BATTLE – *collecting the identification papers from a fallen comrade, Chateau Wood.*

deep outpost line, designed to absorb most of the weight of an attack forward of the main trenches. The withdrawal, codenamed "Operation Alberich", shortened the German line by twenty-five miles, so freeing up fourteen divisions. In their wake, the retreating soldiers operated a scorched earth policy, poisoning wells, raising towns and villages to the ground and leaving hundreds of booby traps to punish the unwary.

The Allies had not planned for this – their spring target was to have been the very positions which the Germans had vacated – so it was decided that the British should make an attack at Arras to draw German troops away from the main focus, which was to be a French assault on the line of the river Aisne.

On 9 April the British attacked at Arras. Fourteen divisions including four Canadian divisions supported by 2,817 guns and forty-eight tanks tore into the defences to a depth of over three miles. The Canadians captured Vimy Ridge and some ten thousand Germans were taken prisoner. Further attacks continued to gain ground and a major German counter-attack on 6 May was driven off with severe casualties. In the last week of May the British VII Corps broke into the first part of the Hindenburg Line in a sector held by depleted divisions, stationed there for a rest.

On 16 April the new French Commander-in-Chief, General Nivelle, who had replaced Joffre after the Battle of Verdun, launched an offensive on the Chemin des Dames. He staked everything on a quick breakthrough but failed to achieve it. The first large-scale attack by French tanks failed tragically; most of the eighty-two Schneider tanks were destroyed. The new German defences proved effective. The sheer weight of the French attack, fifty-two French

BY THE END OF 1916 the British Expeditionary Force had expanded to fifty-six divisions, and for its planned offensives in 1917 it would have twice as many heavy guns as were assembled for the Somme. In the British sector, Haig launched a succession of minor attacks on the Somme to suggest to the Germans that he planned to resume major operations there once the weather improved. Local attacks began on 10 January and there was a three-division assault on 17 February.

German strategy was based in 1917 on the belief that they could no longer withstand another offensive on the scale of the Somme. To reduce pressure on their lines the plan was to remain on the defensive in both East and West, and to abandon many of the positions they had expended so much blood to defend. Early in 1917, the German Army withdrew to defensive positions built the previous year, the "Siegfried-Stellung", known to the British as the "Hindenburg Line". It began near the British front at Arras and ran through Saint Quentin to Laffaux, six miles north-east of Soissons. The Hindenburg Line incorporated every lesson learned in defensive warfare; masses of wire protected concrete strongpoints that formed a

" German strategy was now based on the belief that they could not withstand another offensive on the scale of the Somme. "

divisions against thirty-eight German and a greater preponderance of artillery, captured a few miles of ground and twenty-thousand prisoners in the first four days. Yet by the end of April there was no sign of a breakthrough, and French losses were soaring: it was all very familiar, and for soldiers who had been promised a victory after three years of suffering, it was too much. On 29 April the first mutinies began. Over the next few weeks sixty-eight of France's 112 divisions reported "acts of collective indiscipline" – essentially strikes. Soldiers refused to go back into the line or to make attacks. Pétain was appointed Chief of the General Staff to replace Nivelle, and he set about restoring order and morale, but it was plain that the only Allied army left in the field was that of the British Empire.

The French Army's parlous condition made it difficult for Haig to call an end to the diversionary Arras offensive – which was becoming more bogged down. Between 9 April and 17 May, when the Arras offensive finally ended, the British lost 159,000 men. Haig's true objective was to break through to the Belgian coast and capture the ports of Zeebrugge and Ostend, which were being used as bases by German coastal U-boats. One division (with special tanks) was prepared for an amphibious assault behind the German lines. The first stage of the plan was to attack the southern end of the ridge that dominated the Ypres salient, Messines Ridge.

This assault was put under the command of General Sir Hubert Plumer, Commander of the Second Army, acknowledged as a meticulous and careful military planner. By the time the attack was launched on 21 May, Plumer had undertaken a tunneling operation of unprecedented ambition. Twenty-one mines had been laid below the German front line in tunnels ranging from 200 to more than 2000 feet in length, at depths of fifty to 100 feet.

To start the assault, the British artillery began to bombard the area, their fire increasing from 2 June until 2,266 guns were involved. The tunnels

extending beneath the German lines contained a total of about 450 tons of high explosive and their detonation at 03.10 hrs on 7 June reverberated across the Front and was heard on the southern coast of England. Plumer was recorded as saying to his staff officers the night before the battle that they may not make history, but they would certainly change geography. The German front line vanished in an apocalyptic blast, and seven British divisions, one Australian and one New Zealand, stormed the Ridge, reaching the crest by mid-morning and taking the entire German reserve line over the course of four days' action.

On 31 July, the offensive known to history as the "Third Battle of Ypres", or more commonly "Passchendaele", began. An artillery bombardment had been under way since 18 July and air battles raged overhead as the British and French air forces sought to make the task of the German gunners impossible by destroying their observation balloons and aircraft. On the night of 31 July, the rain began.

The rain that summer was the worst for forty years, a near constant drizzle that filled the craters with muddy slime. The drainage system had been shattered by the weight of the bombardment, and even when it stopped raining, it remained overcast with never enough sunshine to dry out the ground. Soldiers of both sides fought and died in a man-made swamp.

In the early offensives, General Gough's Fifth Army was tasked with breaking through to the north of Ypres in a series of engagements around Langemarck, Pilckem Ridge and Gheluvelt. When these attempts failed, Haig transferred the weight of the offensive to Plumer and the Second Army. In the brief periods of good weather, Plumer consistently managed to make modest advances, inflicting heavy casualties on the enemy in what were known as "bite and hold" tactics.

German counter-attacks were smashed by British

artillery. Haig continued the battle through October and into November when the ruins of the village of Passchendaele came to form the immediate objective, finally being taken by Canadian troops on 6 November. Haig had reports on his desk suggesting German morale was about to crack, but his own army was sorely tried too. Both sides lost approximately a quarter of a million men at Third Ypres.

As the Passchendaele offensive petered out, the British launched a surprise attack on the German lines near Cambrai. Planned by the British Third Army under Sir Julian Byng, the assault was spearheaded by 378 tanks – the first mass tank attack in history.

Cambrai was initially conceived as a raid that would destroy enemy guns and cause confusion and with-draw the same day. By the time it was launched, however, the intention was to make a major break-through, using the tanks and eleven divisions (six infantry and five cavalry). The objective, Cambrai, had become an important railhead.

The attack began at dawn on 20 November with an intense barrage, and the first two lines were taken by noon. By nightfall 179 tanks were out of action but the forward troops had advanced five miles on a six-mile front. This initial success was the product of new artillery methods that dispensed with the usual lengthy bombardment that gave the enemy time to bring up his reserves. The following week was spent deepening the salient, particularly the heights of Bourlon Wood, which controlled the Bapaume – Cambrai road, but by the end of the month it had become clear that Cambrai could not be encircled from the south, reserves could not be brought up quickly enough and the cavalry could not break out. As had so often been the case before,

the gains had not been sufficiently consolidated, and on the 30th the Germans counter-attacked with twenty divisions. By 3 December they had effectively retaken all the land that the British had won. The British had suffered 50,000 casualties to the Germans' 45,000.

Whilst the British were fighting in Cambrai, matters were coming to a head in Russia. Dissatisfaction had given way to revolution. In February 1917 shortages of food and fuel prompted riots in the streets of Petrograd (formerly St Petersburg), and order collapsed as troops sent in to quell the violent demonstrations sided with the rioters. By mid-March, the entire 170,000-man Russian garrison had mutinied and with no force with which to hold control, Nicholas II abdicated under increasing pressure from his generals and ministers. In the absence of any successor, a Provisional Government took over – but its power was steadily diluted by the influence of the Petrograd Soviet. Germany was anxious to exacerbate the unrest, and permitted the Bolshevik leader, Lenin, to travel through Sweden to reach Petrograd.

The morale of the soldiers on the Eastern Front had plummeted during the summer of 1917. When German forces took Riga in September, their resistance collapsed. Lenin's Bolsheviks overthrew the Provisional Government in October and immediately sought an armistice with Germany. This came into effect on 17 December, and over the winter of 1917–18, as Russian troops laid down their arms, up to forty German divisions were freed up to face the Allies on the Western Front. British forces, however, were already subject to heavy demands. In Italy, on 24 October, the Austro-Hungarians, heavily reinforced by German troops, launched a major offensive along the Isonzo front, known as the Battle of Caporetto.

" The rain that summer was the worst for forty years, a near constant drizzle that filled the craters with muddy slime. "

German heavy artillery destroyed the Italian positions, sending the Italians into retreat, eventually forming a line just twenty miles from Venice. The Italians lost 10,000 killed, 30,000 wounded and over 265,000 taken prisoner, and they called on the British and French for reinforcements – not to counter-attack, but simply to hold the line.

As Russia faced revolution and Italy sought help, the Allies had, at least, gained one new partner in 1917, On 6 April, the United States had entered the fray. Germany's unrestricted U-boat campaign in the North Atlantic finally provoked President Woodrow Wilson into asking Congress to declare war, and America joined the Allied side as an "Associated Power". At this point, America had only a small professional Army – their troops would not be available in force until later in 1918. However, Congress passed a Selective Service Act in May, and in June, the 1st US Infantry Division arrived in France. The boost to Allied morale was significant. With the promise of vast numbers of reinforcements on the Allied side, Germany now had one last opportunity to win the war, before the odds became insurmountable.

Below
US troops shortly after their arrival in France.

A GROUP OF PATIENTS, many of whom are amputees, at Roehampton House. These men lost their limbs through enemy action. Others lost their limbs for different reasons.

" WE HAD A TREMENDOUS number of frostbite cases at the beginning of 1917. Their feet were absolutely white, swollen up, dead. Some of their toes dropped off with it. "

British VAD nurse Kathleen Yardwood

THE HARRODIANS – a football team of female employees from Harrods department store.

OFFICERS IN TRAINING at the Royal Military College, Sandhurst, 1917. In the lounge before the start of a rugby game.

WOMEN'S ARMY AUXILIARY CORPS (THE WAAC'S), drilling in Hyde Park.

By early 1918, there were over 6,000 WAAC's in France.

THE FIRST AID NURSING Yeomanry – the FANYs. A group of ambulance drivers in Calais, fur-coated against the January cold.

MEN OF THE BLACK WATCH celebrating New Year's Day in the hutments at Henencourt, 1917.

Opposite
A SOLDIER HAS A TOOTH "extracted" using a large pair of tongs.

❝ **WE DIDN'T HAVE DENTISTS** in any great number until 1916. Then when the dentists came over and the men got their teeth put right, and the dead ones pulled out and so on, it certainly got them into another era of health, because their food could then be properly digested. It seems a small thing, but it was of tremendous value. ❞

Lieutenant Godfrey Buxton, Royal Army Medical Corps

SECURING SCALING LADDERS in British trenches on 8 April 1917 – the day before the Battle of Arras. The design and steepness of these ladders illustrate the difficulty soldiers had in even getting out of the trenches for an attack. It made many a sitting target as they went "over the top".

THE TAKING OF VIMY RIDGE in April 1917 – Canadian soldiers advance alongside
a tank across No Man's Land.

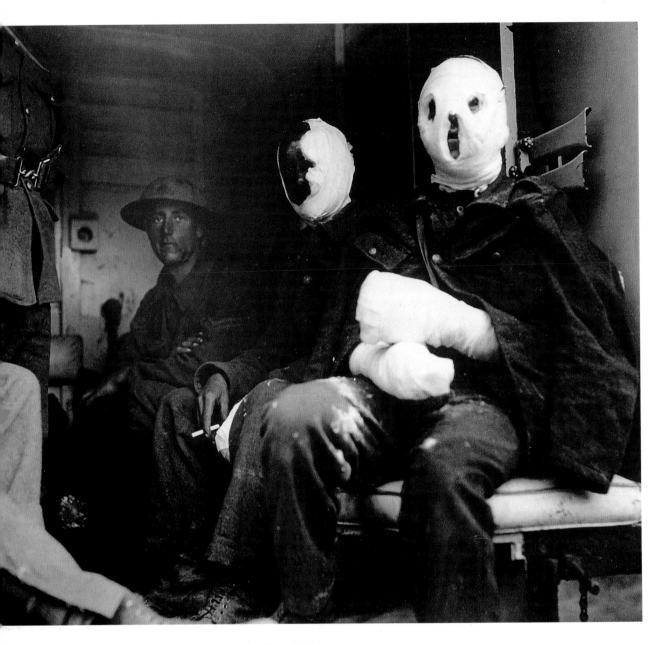

WOUNDED CANADIANS en route back to Blighty.

Opposite
A NEW ZEALAND CHAPLAIN celebrating Holy Communion
in a field near the front line in France, 1917.

❝ FROM A PRACTICAL POINT of view there was no religion in the front line,
although our unit padre used to come and visit us quite a lot. But he was never
allowed to stay in one place too long because he got in the way. Behind the line
there were the usual church services and then there was a church parade on a
Sunday, in which the whole battalion sang lusty hymns to a wheezy harmonium
and the padre preached a sermon that you couldn't hear anyhow. ❞

Private Norman Demuth

THE ARRRAS OFFENSIVE. 9.2-inch Howitzers of the 91st Battery, Royal Garrison
Artillery, in action near Arras, 1 April 1917.

Opposite
BRITISH TROOPS in a reserve trench awaiting orders to move forward during the
Battle of Arras, near Tilloy, 10 April, 1917.

❝ ARRAS WAS THE FIRST time I went over the top. We played football together
as we went over. That was the tradition in the East Surreys. I remember the ball
dropping at my feet and I passed it to Captain Maxwell. 'That was a good pass
you made, young Withers!' he shouted, before he thumped it towards the
German lines. ❞

Cecil Withers, East Surrey Regiment

PREPARATION FOR THE BATTLE OF ARRAS, 1917. 12th Division Artillery Officers observing fire and Royal Engineer field telephonists passing back results.

" **WHEN ZERO HOUR** came at Arras, the first wave went off. As soon as it came in sight of the Hun, the massacre commenced, the enemy lining his parapet and shooting our boys like rabbits. "

E.J. Rule, 14th Battalion, Australian Imperial Force

" THE BRITISH ATTACK came to a standstill. We waited for several regiments of cavalry to sweep up and drive us towards Berlin. But this didn't happen, much to our surprise. **"**

A German NCO

" I GOT WOUNDED at the end of that battle. I was temporarily blinded in one eye, but it could have been worse. At the end of the battle I lay bleeding in a trench. There was blood coming out of my eye – pouring out all over my face. My head looked blown in. They thought I was dead and they were going to bury me. I was in a half-conscious state, and I can remember a soldier getting hold of me and saying, 'Here – this bloke's alive!' That man saved my life. I'd have been buried alive in Arras if it hadn't been for him. "

Cecil Withers

BRITISH SOLDIERS lie dead after the Battle of Arras.

Opposite
EXHAUSTED AFTER THE BATTLE OF ARRAS – troops climb aboard requisitioned London buses. They will be taken behind the lines where they will have a chance to recover.

❝ I REMEMBER THE FOOD. Mostly we had Fray Bentos corned beef and dog biscuits, as we used to call them. They were terribly hard so you had to soften them with water. And there was Maconochies' stew maybe once a month. We got bread sometimes – and water, and what they called tea for breakfast, lunch and supper. In the reserve we used to get to sit down at a table, but the food was just the same as in the trenches. **❞**

Cecil Withers, East Surrey Regiment

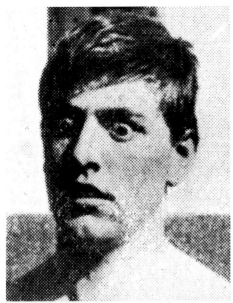

Opposite
BRITISH OFFICERS behind the sandbags, lunching from their mess tins.

Right
SHELL-SHOCKED SOLDIER. His expression is frozen in horror. It is difficult to imagine what this man has witnessed.

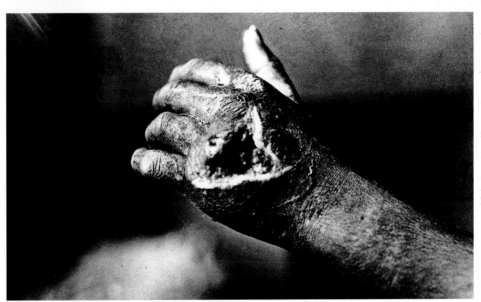

❝ THE FIRST HUT I CAME TO was occupied by men who all had wounds through the palms of their hands. We came to the conclusion they must have held theirs arms up above the trench so that they could be shot through the hand and get invalided home. ❞

Captain Maberly, RAMC

Opposite

A BRITISH SOLDIER uses a hollow tree trunk as camouflage to observe no-man's-land above the level of the trench.

BATTLE ON THE AISNE, 6-27 April 1917. Two sentries in a German advance post with hand-grenades at the ready.

"I CURSE A SAPPER BESIDE ME. He eyes me vacantly – for he is dead. More and more shells, two of them right in our midst. Shrieks of agony and groans all around me. I am splashed with blood. Surely I am hit, for my head feels as though a battering ram has hit it. But no, I appear not to be, although all about me are bits of men and ghastly mixtures of cloth and blood. "

Anthony R. Hossack, Queen Victoria Rifles

THE ROAD NEAR SOISSON, littered with dead bodies after the Battle of the Aisne, May 1917.

BATTLE OF MESSINES – officers of the Innskilling Fusiliers with souvenirs of the capture of Wytschaete village, 12 June.

Opposite
BATTLE OF YPRES – laying a railway line near Boesinghe, 28 July.

Overleaf
MEN OF THE 11th Durham Light Infantry being taken forward by light railway, passing Elverdinghe, 31 July 1917.

DEAD SCOTTTISH SOLDIERS awaiting burial.

Opposite
BATTLE OF PILCKEM RIDGE – stretcher-bearers carrying
a wounded man through knee-deep mud near Boesinghe
1 August 1917.

" AT PILCKEM RIDGE I can still see the bewilderment and fear on the men's faces when we went over the top. All over the battlefield, the wounded were lying there – English and German, all asking for help. We weren't like the Good Samaritan in the Bible – we were the robbers who passed by and left them. You couldn't help them. I came across a Cornishman, ripped from shoulder to waist with shrapnel, his stomach on the ground beside him in a pool of blood. **"**

Private Harry Patch, Cornwall's Light Infantry

BATTLE OF PILCKEM RIDGE –
struggling to prise a field gun out of the
mud, North of Ypres, 2 August 1917.

❝ **THEN WE BROUGHT** up a gun and with great difficulty
got it off the road on to the first part of the route. Then we
had to get it from there past other shell holes ... it took a
long time, but we did eventually get one of our guns about
thirty yards from the road.' An eventual withdrawal with
all the guns proved even worse: 'Time after time they toiled
with these heavy guns, which kept slipping sideways and
getting caught in the mud, and it was a very long time
before we were able to get any of them back on to the
road and away. ❞

Captain E. W. Stoneham, Royal Artillery

BATTLE OF PILCKEM RIDGE – pack mules of the 36th Division passing a wrecked artillery limber and dead mules on the road at St Jean, 31 July.

" I ONCE SAW A MULE that had been killed by an explosion. Our cook tried to break the routine of hard tack biscuits and bully beef by seizing the remains of the mule and frying it up. God only knows what we were eating, but it tasted good. "

Albert "Smiler" Marshall, Essex Yeomanry

AUSTRALIAN WOUNDED on the Menin Road, returning from the front.

ADVANCED RED CROSS DRESSING STATION near Hill 60 treating wounded Australian troops, 26 August 1917.

Below

SCOTTISH SOLDIER guarding captured German officers outside their dug-out near Langemark, October 1917.

Opposite

JOHN (BARNEY) HINES, an Anzac soldier, after the battle of Polygon Wood:

Known as the "souvenir king", he was born in Liverpool, of Irish descent. He served in the Boxer Rebellion in China, before seeing action in the Boer War. He then emigrated to Australia, where at the outbreak of the Great War, despite being aged over forty, he succeeded in joining the Army. Once at the Western front he refused to use a rifle, preferring to carry two sandbags of hand grenades. As a result of his penchant for taking items from German corpses, the Kaiser placed Hines on his personal wanted list. Nevertheless he survived the War.

DEAD AND WOUNDED Australians and Germans in the railway
cutting on Broodeseinde Ridge during the Battle of Passchendaele,
12 October 1917.

A BRITISH SOLDIER covering a dead German on the fire step of a
trench during the capture of Ovillers.

A GERMAN SOLDIER closes the eyes of a fallen comrade near Havringcourt.

❝ WHILE AT ARMENTIÈRES I was detailed to form part of a firing squad at the execution of a deserter. He was tied to a post in his civilian clothes and we were told to fire at a piece of white cloth pinned over his heart. ❞

Rifleman Henry Williamson, London Rifle Brigade

BETWEEN 1914 AND 1920, the British Army executed 346 British and Commonwealth soldiers for a variety of offences, including desertion, cowardice and murder. Spies were also shot – as seen above.

BATTLE OF CAMBRAI – men of the 11th Leicester Regiment with machine guns in a captured second-line trench, Ribecourt, 20 November.

Opposite

Private Theo Leslie Seabrook (left), 2nd Lieutenant William Keith Seabrook, seen here as a sergeant (centre), and Private George Ross Seabrook. The three brothers, of Fivedock, New South Wales, Australia, were all serving with the 17th Battalion, Australian Imperial Forces when they were killed together at Polygon Wood in the Ypres Salient on 20-21 September 1917. At the time of their deaths, George was 25, Theo 24 and William 21. Theo and George, who have no known grave, are commemorated on the Menin Gate at Ypres, while William is buried at Lijssenthoek Military Cemetery.

THE ONSET OF THE TANKS at Cambrai was overwhelming. The triple belts of German wire were crossed as if they had been beds of nettles and 350 pathways were sheared through them for the infantry. The defenders of the front trenches, scrambling out of the dug-outs and shelters, saw the leading tanks almost upon them... As these tanks swung left-handed and fired down into the trenches, other tanks appeared in multitudes behind them out of the mist. **"**

Captain D.G. Browne, Tank Corps

Opposite

BATTLE OF CAMBRAI. British troops with a donkey and cart found in captured Ribecourt, 29 November 1917.

EXTRICATING A HORSE which had been blown into a ditch by a shell-burst, near Reutel, 5 October.

" WE USED HORSES FOR ALMOST everything: pulling supplies, food, ammunition, bringing back the dead and wounded, and God knows there were plenty of them. There was hardly any motor transport and the animals suffered terribly in that war. "

Private Fred Lloyd, Veterinary Corps

EN ROUTE TO FRANCE, a cheering group of American soldiers
lifts anchor and heads to France to participate in the Great War.

AN EXUBERANT AMERICAN SOLDIER sees the humour in gas-mask drill.

DRESSED TO THRILL, a soldier has make-up applied by another while touring with the Canadian Concert Party, *The Maple Leaves*.

" **PHOTOGRAPHS OF ME** in my glamour girl's things brought me a nice little income. Especially if I'd signed them. The troops loved them. "

Corporal Tommy Keele, 12th Divisional Concert Party

CHRISTMAS ENTERTAINMENT – a pantomime horse

1918

- GERMANY'S SPRING OFFENSIVE
- OPERATION MICHAEL
- BATTLE OF AMIENS
- AMERICANS IN ACTION
- THE ARMISTICE

BATTLE OF EPHEY – *wounded and prisoners coming in.*
A wounded "bantam" (a term for a soldier of less-than-average height)
is assisted by a somewhat taller German prisoner.

THE COMMANDERS OF THE GERMAN ARMY, Hindenburg and Ludendorff, knew that although the British and French armies had been substantially weakened by the battles of 1917 and calls by Italy for support, fresh American troops were beginning to flood across the Atlantic and could decisively turn the tide in on the Western Front, should the war be allowed to drag on.

Following the collapse of Russia in the east, they were able to transfer many of their divisions to the Western Front, and enjoy a temporary numerical advantage over the western Allies, with 192 divisions against 169.

The commanders set about reorganizing the German Army to maximize their chances. The youngest and fittest soldiers were concentrated in special "attack" divisions, while the oldest and weakest men were relegated to second-line divisions, only really capable of static defence. New tactics were introduced too, with the assaults being led by newly formed battalions of stormtroopers equipped with light machine guns, flame-throwers and hand-grenades. They were elite troops, trained to move quickly to isolate pockets of resistance which would then be

mopped up by the follow-up troops. The artillery had also been revolutionized through the work of Colonel Georg Bruchmüller who devised a gas-shell-laced drumfire bombardment system that had effectively suppressed defences on the Eastern Front. Many of these tactics had been tested during the German counter-attack at Cambrai the previous November, but they were now to be implemented across the entire front.

The Allies, too, were reorganizing and strengthening their defences at the start of the year. The plan was to emulate the German system of defence in depth, where there were three zones – forward, battle and rear. These zones were set out as separate systems, consisting of lines of trenches, strongpoints and machine-gun emplacements, designed to provide all-round defence. Unfortunately, the troops were unaccustomed to the new system and placed too much weight in the forward zone. This was undoubtedly a contributory factor in the outcome of the next stage of the war.

It was Ludendorff's plan to launch a series of interlinked offensives to split the British and French armies. The BEF should be driven back towards the Channel coast, and weakened; the French might be forced to sue for a settlement. The overall assault, named Kaiserschlacht – the emperor's battle – would begin with Operation Michael, targeting the British Fifth Army under Gough.

On 21 March the British Fifth Army was subjected to the most intensive artillery fire of the war – 6,600 guns pummelled the British positions and an early morning fog meant that the stormtroopers leading the German attack were on top of the British before they knew what was happening. The attack broke down in several places where the fog lifted or local

> *" By 24 March the Germans had advanced fourteen miles, the greatest advance on the Western front since 1914. "*

resistance was well coordinated, but the line was penetrated to considerable depth elsewhere. Some units were surrounded. Others were compelled to fall back. By 24 March the Germans had advanced fourteen miles, the greatest advance on the Western Front since 1914.

Under such pressure, the Fifth Army's resistance collapsed, exposing the Third Army's flank and forcing it to withdraw, abandoning Peronne and the Cambrai salient. Pressing home their advantage, the German Eighteenth Army drove the remnants of the Third Army across the Somme before British or French support units were able to move in. Paris itself came under artillery fire on 25 March, and to consolidate command, Foch was made overall Allied Commander, being officially named Commander in Chief of all Allied forces in France on 3 April.

The British were driven back to the old battlefields of the Somme. However, if the British were experiencing some disagreeably familiar sights, the Germans were staggered at what they discovered. British supply dumps were packed with foodstuffs not seen in Germany for years. Told that the Allies were on their last legs, the Germans were to find their enemies living in what was, by comparison, the lap of luxury.

The perennial problem faced by attacking forces on the Western Front was how to advance over a battlefield, even if the enemy withdrew. The great artillery pieces that destroyed all before them were mostly horse-drawn, and to get them across the churned-up fields they created required new roads, if not railways.

Hampered by transport problems, Operation Michael was called off, with significant losses to both sides. Many elite German stormtroopers were sacrificed without making any great gains. Casualty figures listed 163,000 British, 77,000 French and 250,000 Germans. Given these heavy losses, General Gough was relieved of command and replaced by General Sir Henry Rawlinson.

The next phase of Ludendorff's offensive, Operation Georgette, was scheduled for 28 March. It would be an attack near Arras, intended to drive all the way to the Channel coast at Boulogne, seventy-two miles up the road. Preceded by an equally ferocious barrage, nine German divisions attacked four British divisions, but were stopped in their tracks. Although a thrust at Amiens made better progress, the Germans were compelled to admit the failure of their offensive on 5 April.

Ninety thousand British and French soldiers had been taken prisoner during the great German offensive. However, the Germans persevered, launching another, smaller-scale assault near Ypres on 9 April. Again the British were driven back, prompting Haig's famous Order of the Day on the tenth: "With our backs to the wall and believing in the justice of our cause each one must fight to the end. The safety of our homes and the freedom of mankind alike depend upon the conduct of each one of us at this critical moment."

Plumer returned from Italy to take command of the Second Army once more, and was forced to retire from the hard-won ground at Passchendaele in order to hold the line. Further German assaults took place on the Somme on 24 April, where Villers-Bretonneux fell and was retaken by a prompt counter-attack that involved the war's first (and only) tank versus tank engagement – thirteen tanks a side with the British winning this particular battle.

Ludendorff changed tack and looked south, launching an assault against French positions on 27 May, as part of Operation Blücher. The chosen battlefield was the Chemin des Dames. On the opening day of the assault, three British divisions, already damaged by recent offensives to the north and sent south to recuperate, were all but destroyed. These divisions, along with the French XI Corps, were forced down the ridges of the Chemin des Dames. A day later two more British divisions were overwhelmed, and the German Seventh Army seized the bridges controlling the river Anise and its canal. This brought them within reach of the cities of Reims and Poisson, on either side of salient 25 miles wide and eleven miles deep. In three days the Germans advanced forty miles, and over the coming weeks, as they pushed deeper into the Champagne region, German troops took Poisson, and soon were back on the banks of the Marne, the high water mark of their 1914 campaign.

The mood of crisis in the Allied camp was grave – but then the American 2nd and 3rd Divisions joined in the defence of the French line. General Foch blocked a direct attack towards Paris and senior commanders on both sides began to recognize that Germany had shot its bolt. Furthermore, German advances had driven deep salient in the old front line, almost doubling the length of front that the much-reduced German Army had to occupy. Ludendorff persevered, however, launching a further assault, codenamed Gneisenau, to push forward between Noyon and Montdidier – which was blocked by the French, and his next attack on either side of Reims met with even stronger resistance. On 15 July, the German Army converged on the French First Army, over a massive 26-mile front – and before the morning was over they had been stopped in their tracks.

Despite small gains by the German Seventh and Ninth Armies to the south west, their advantage was short-lived as 36 divisions of British, French, American and Italian troops united to drive 52 German divisions into retreat. The tide was beginning to turn.

On 18 July, the Allies launched a counter-attack and eliminated the Marne salient, making a five-mile advance on the first day. Soissons was retaken on 2 August, and a day later the German Army was in retreat to the Vesle and Aisne rivers.

The British Army lost a thousand artillery pieces in the retreats of 1918, but so massive was British industrial superiority that they were replaced by the summer. By this time, however, the Germans had lost 793 guns and Ludendorff was close to nervous collapse. The events of the next day were, he owned, a "black day of the German Army". On 8 August the British attacked and smashed through the German front line at Amiens to a depth of eight miles.

Even if the later assaults between 9 and 11 August failed to match the advances of the first day, the German Army suffered 75,000 casualties compared with only 22,000 for the British. The British success was due largely to the commanders' grasp of combined-arms warfare which would typify all future operations, with the Royal Air Force providing close air support for the advancing tanks and infantry.

The tide had also turned in Italy and the recovered Italian Army under General Armando Diaz, heavily reinforced by British and French forces, launched an all-out offensive at Vittorio Veneto on 24 October leading to a collapse in the Austrian position. The Italians suffered some 38,000 casualties, while the Austro-Hungarians lost 300,000 taken prisoner and they signed an armistice on 3 November, leaving Germany as the only surviving member of the Central Powers.

Returning to the Western Front, the Allied command realized they had a good chance of finishing the war in 1918 and, to that end, the supreme commander Marshal Foch proposed a series of rolling offensives by all the combatant powers to keep the Germans off balance and always moving backwards – tout le monde à la bataille, ("everyone into battle"). Prior to

« The Kaiser abdicated on 9 November, and the armistice came into effect at eleven o'clock in the morning of 11 November in the eleventh hour of the eleventh day of the eleventh month. »

this, early September saw the first independent action by an American Army of the war, with the First US Army clearing the St Mihiel salient. Following this, the first major assault on the German position was carried out in the Meuse–Argonne by French and American forces on 26 September. This was followed by a British offensive around Cambrai on 27 September and a joint Anglo-Belgian assault between Lys and the sea on 28 September then, finally, an attack on the Hindenburg Line near St Quentin by the British Fourth Army on the 29th. These four major assaults met varying degrees of success – the performance of the most northerly offensive was particularly weak – but they all succeeded in pushing back the Germans whose reserves could not be moved with sufficient speed from one threatened area to another.

Ludendorff had been convinced of the need for an armistice since August, but the terms offered were unacceptable to him and he resigned on 26 October. The Allies kept up the pressure throughout the end of October. Germany requested an armistice on 3 November, thus averting an Allied offensive across the German frontier. The Kaiser abdicated on 9 November, and the armistice came into effect at eleven o'clock in the morning of 11 November – "the eleventh hour of the eleventh day of the eleventh month"– and the war was over.

Below
A rare head-on combat photograph, showing the action of a man about to hurl a potato masher grenade. Taken at Villers-Bretonneux in April, as Hindenburg's 18th Army overran Allied lines near the Somme.

GERMAN OFFENSIVE IN PICARDY, March 1918. German infantry
advancing through the village of Templeux, passing a horse transport
supply column.

ON THE 20TH MARCH we got the order, tomorrow morning the attack will start – we got a high feeling. We were in high spirits because we hoped for our victory in this battle.

Major Hartwig Pohlman, 36th Prussian Division

GERMAN TROOPS ADVANCE in the sector near Villers-Bretonneux during Germany's last major effort to secure victory on the Western Front.

THE FIRST AMERICAN DEAD – the
Pioneer Regiment, March 1918.

❝ WE PASSED DEAD OF BOTH ARMIES, but many more
Boche than Americans. I was surprised at the indifference
I felt toward dead Americans - they seemed a perfectly
natural thing to come across, and I felt absolutely no
shudder go down my back as I would have, had I seen
the same thing a year ago. ❞

Lieutenant Phelps Harding, American Expeditionary Force, in a letter, 1918

" ON THE FIRESTEP in the trenches during the night, you could
hear the groaning of the dying – but you couldn't go out to help them.
There were rats feeding on their flesh. They were dying there, dying
in misery and pain, and the rats were nibbling away at their flesh. "

Private Cecil Withers, 17th Battalion, Royal Fusiliers

I USED TO THINK, 'Shall we get through tomorrow or shall we get a packet? Am I going up the line tonight; will I be coming back? It's dark and everything may be quiet now, but am I going to see the sun coming up in the morning? And when the sun comes up in the morning, shall I see it set at night?' **"**

Private Harry Patch, Duke of Cornwall's Light Infantry

CAPTURED BRITISH SOLDIERS are allowed by their German guards to salvage the personal effects of comrades killed in battle, for inventory and eventual return to the men's families.

A GERMAN PRISONER OF WAR camp. The two men tied to a post
are British prisoners who have stolen some soup from the prison
stores. Two unconcerned German officers pass by in the foreground.

AT THE GUARDS DIVISION sports at Bavincourt, 30 June 1918,
the Duke of Connaught grins as he watches...

. . . SOLDIERS PILLOW-FIGHTING on a log.

Overleaf

ZULU TROOPS OF THE SOUTH AFRICAN ARMY on the Western
Front giving a ceremonial performance, away from the Front Line.

AN OFFICER enjoys a cigar with two small companions, Neulette,
26 August 1918.

THE NEW TECHNOLOGY MEETS THE OLD: a carrier pigeon is released from a small aperture in the side of a tank.

FLY-BLOWN GERMAN corpses by a machine gun emplacement, Meteren, July 1918.

AN AMERICAN FIELD ARTILLERY TEAM reloading a cannon.

THE BATTLE OF TARDENOIS – 1/5th Devons capture a German
in the Bois de Rheims.

TRIUMPHANT OFFICERS AND MEN of New Zealand Division
celebrate the capture of Grevillers atop a German 4.2 battery.

❝ THE POOR THINGS – burnt and blistered all over with great mustard-coloured suppurating blisters, with blind eyes, all sticky and stuck together, and always fighting for breath, with voices a mere whisper, saying that their throats are closing and they know they will choke. **❞**

A nurse

BRITISH SOLDIERS in shell hole, Mont Kemmel, 2 September 1918.

U.S. SERVICEMEN say their farewell as they leave Winchester and begin their journey
to the Western front.

OUTFITTING BLACK AMERICAN RECRUITS at Camp Meade. Black American troops could take pride in their wartime achievements. 367,000 served in the U.S. armed forces of whom 130,000 served in France. The 93rd Division served side-by-side with the French and won numerous awards. The first two Americans to win France's highest decoration, the Croix de Guerre were black and 171 black soldiers were awarded the Legion d'Honneur.

AMERICAN TROOPS hold an outpost in the Vosges with a French automatic rifle.

Opposite
AN AMERICAN GUN CREW firing a 37-mm gun during an advance on German positions in late 1918.

“ YOU TALKED TO YOUR MATES in the gun crew. At some point you showed your emotions. That was why our comradeship was so important – because I was scared more or less all the time I was out there. ”

Private Harry Patch

A GROUP OF GERMAN PRISONERS are marched along a French road.

Opposite
THE 8TH LIVERPOOL IRISH Regiment, 57th Division entering Lille with one proud boy, 18 October 1918.

DEAD GERMAN GUNNER in a machine gun nest at Villers Devy Dun Sassey, France. He was killed on the same day as the poet, Wilfred Owen – November 4, 1918.

" I AM THE ENEMY YOU KILLED, MY FRIEND.

I knew you in this dark: for so you frowned
Yesterday through me as you jabbed and killed.
I parried; but my hands were loath and cold.
Let us sleep now... "

Lieutenant Wilfred Owen, M.C., 2nd Battalion, Manchester Regiment

THE COLONEL and men of the 9th East Surreys celebrating the armistice at St Wasst, near Baval, 11th November 1918.

" AT THE ARMISTICE I was in a trench, and the Germans opposite got out of theirs, bowed to us and walked off, and that was it. There was nothing to celebrate with – except biscuits. "

Corporal John Oborne, 4th Battalion, Devonshire Regiment

EXCITED LONDONERS cheering in the streets and from atop a double-decker bus, after news of the signing of the Armistice is heard.

❝ ON ARMISTICE DAY, we paraded round the garden in our night clothes blowing anything that we could blow and banging anything bangable – such as a tea tray. ❞

Eleven year old English boy, Desmond Flower

AFTERMATH

● SOLDIER'S HOMECOMING

● HEALING THE WOUNDS

● FUNERAL OF THE UNKNOWN WARRIOR

KING GEORGE V *in a horse-drawn carriage at the Epsom Derby, being pursued by an ex-soldier.*

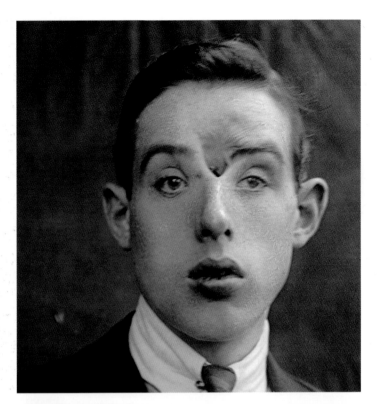

A BRITISH SOLDIER wounded between the eyes by a piece of time-fuse which lodged at the back of his cheek. It was extracted by massage without further injury to the face. *(Below)* The same patient, after a plate was made for his spectacles to cover the wound. The surgeon was Captain Derwent Wood, RA.

CAPTAIN DERWENT WOOD, finishing the plate of a patient's face. *(Bottom)* He puts the final touches to the plate.

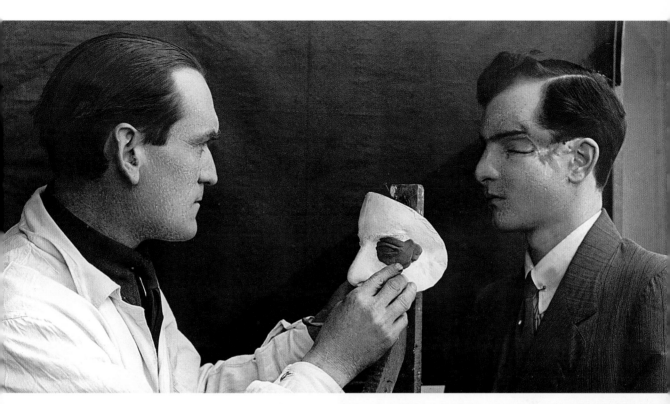

AN ARTIFICIAL limb workshop at Roehampton.

CONVALESCENT GERMAN AMPUTEES taking exercise on the parade ground at their military hospital.

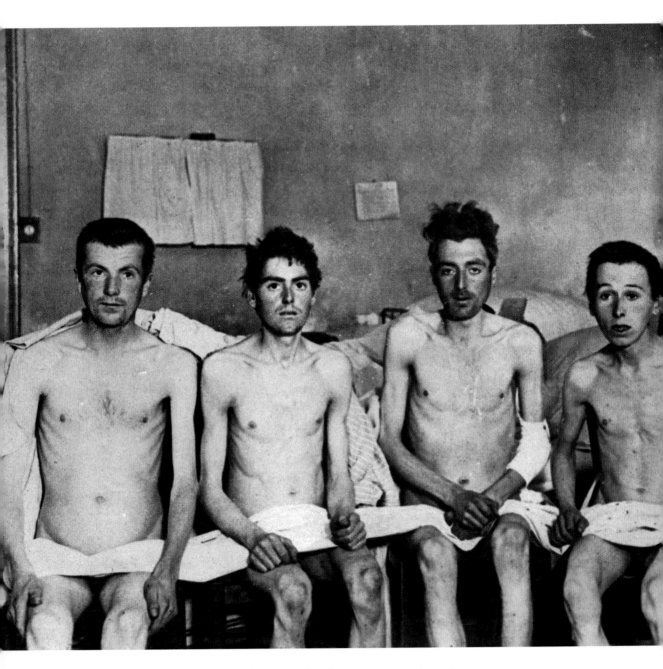

BRITISH SOLDIERS suffering from disease and malnutrition were released from a German prison camp under the terms of the Armistice.

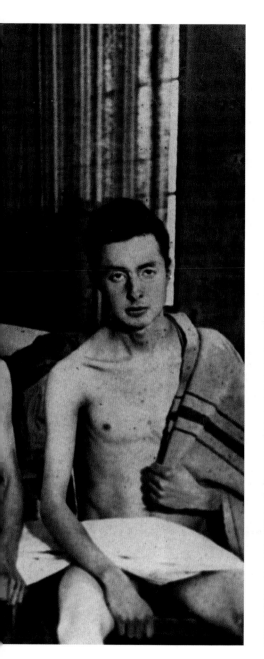

A LAND FIT FOR HEROES. Like so many of the men who went out to fight and die for their King and country, the peacetime reward for this man and his family was unemployment, hunger and despair.

THESE MEN fell at the edge of a wood near Nannevous, where they lay until the following year's thaw revealed their shattered bodies.

THE BODY OF THE UNKNOWN WARRIOR is transported back to Britain from France, 1920.

THE VIMY WAR Memorial under construction in France.

Right above
THE UNVEILING BY KING GEORGE V of the Cenotaph in London's Whitehall.

Right
IN JUNE 2001, TWENTY BODIES WERE UNEARTHED near Arras. The skeletons lie arm-in-arm and are still wearing their boots. They are the men of the Grimsby Chums, perhaps some of the same men pictured in their cloth caps on page 41 of this book. They all died together on Easter Monday 1917. They are just some of the threequarters of a million British men who perished in the Great War. "Their Name Liveth Evermore"

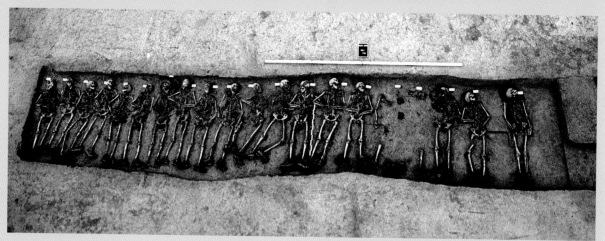

index

A

Aisne, Battle of the 207, 208-9
Albert, Battle of 137, 142-3, 146
AMERICAN ARMY
   black recruits 263
   casualties 244-5
   engagements' description
      240, 241
   enters war 183
   field artillery 256-7
   gas mask drill 233
   leaving for France 232
   leaving Winchester 262
   machine gun crew 264-5
   outpost, Vosges 264
   play acting 233
   YMCA canteen 255
Argyll and Sutherland
   Highlanders 67, 92-3,
   100-1
Arkwright, Lt 60
armistice
   background 241
   East Surrey Regiment 270
   London street 271
   released British prisoners of
      war 278-9
Arras, First Battle of 192, 196-9,
   200-1, 202-3
   description 180-1
Artois, Battle of 77
Aubers Ridge, Battle of 77, 97
Auchonvillers 176
AUSTRALIAN ARMY
   advanced dressing station
      219
   Anzac Cove landing 106
   casualties 111
   casualties at Broodeseinde
      Ridge 222
   three brothers 227
   wounded on Menin Road
      218-19
Aveluy 154, 158-9

B

Bazentine-le-Grand 152-3
Beaumont-Hamel 115, 116, 143

Black Watch 190
Blenheim Palace 118
Bouzincourt 160
Britain
   factory workers 34-5
   Harrods female footballers
      186
   recruitment posters 74-5
   ship-building workers
      120
BRITISH ARMY
   behind the front 54, 55, 69
   behind the lines, luxury of a
      bath 161
   Boulogne Quay 53
   casualties on road near
      Soisson 208-9
   casualties' property 157
   communication trench 137
   conscription 114
   enlistment 32-3, 36-7
   Expeditionary Force [BEF] 43-
      5, 49, 52, 53, 76-7
   firing squad 224-5
   first black officer 130
   front line living conditions
      90
   medical condition 82-3
   medical examinations 36-7,
      130-1
   medical impact of gas 101
   New Year's Day 1917: 190
   pre war 23, 25
   recruitment 49, 82
   recruits, Bermondsey 82-3
   reservists called-up 43
   resting in bombed out
      building 174-5
   scaling ladders 192
   shell hole, Mount Kemmel
      261
   Territorial Force pre-war 25
   trench warfare 94, 127, 128-9
   volunteers 32-3
BRITISH ARMY CASUALTIES
   artificial limb workshop 276
   Chateau Wood 179
   dead bodies concealed by
      snow, Nannevous 280

dead, condition before
   burial 97
Ephey, Battle of 236-7
First Battle of Arras 202
funeral December 1914: 73
gas victims 260-1
knee-deep mud 215
prisoners of war 248-9
Roehampton House 184-5
Scottish dead 214
trenches 246-7
wounded amputees 184-5
wounded face repair 274-5
wounded waiting for train
   December 1914: 72
wounded, Battle of the
   Somme 148-9
wounded, Blenheim Palace
   118
wounded, Buckingham
   Palace 119
wounded, Dernancourt 164-5
BRITISH ARMY TRAINING
   Cambridge University 38
   Crowborough 40
   Eton College 38-9
   Hampstead 84
   Lincolnshire Regiment 41
   Royal Military College rugby
      match 186-7
   Saffron Walden 85
British military cemetery 156
British poverty post-war
   families 279
British poverty pre-war
   East End 1912: 13
   families 13, 14-15
   tin bath 16-17
British privilege pre-war
   Cambridge University
      recruits 38
   Eton College Training Corps
      38-9
   Eton vs Harrow 12-13, 17
Bruchmüller, Col Georg 238
Brussels 140
Buckingham Palace 119
Byng, General Sir Julian
   182

C

Cambrai, Battle of 226-7,
   228-9
   description 182
Cambridge University recruits
   38
camouflage 110, 206
Canadian army
   casualties 194
   concert party 234
   Somme, Battle of the 145
   Vimy Ridge 192-3
Caporetto, Battle of 182-3
Carney 162
Cenotaph unveiling 283
chaplains 195
Chaplin, Mrs Eric 12-13
Chemin des Dames, Battle of
   239-40
CHRISTMAS
   1914 49, 51
   1914 fraternization 50, 70-1
   1914 London Rifle Brigade 68
   1916 mistletoe and pudding
      177
   1917 pantomime horse 235
Churchill, Winston 78-9
civilian casualties, children
   104-5
combined-arms warfare 240
Connaught, HRH Duke of 250

D

Dardanelles campaign
   description 78-9
death, fear of 134, 247
defence systems description
   238
Derby Scheme, The 76
Devonshire Regiment 258
Driscole, Drummer 87
Durham Light Infantry 212-13

E

East Surrey Regiment 270, 86,
   197
Ephey, Battle of 236-7

Eton College Training Corps 38-9

Eton vs Harrow 12-13, 17

Eton wall game 14

F

Falkenhayn, General Erich von 50, 114

FANYs, Calais 189

firing squads 103, 244-5

flame-throwers 99

Foch, Marshal Ferdinand 239, 240

food 204-5

Fosse 8: 78

Franz Ferdinand, Archduke 26

fraternization 50, 70-1, 124

FRENCH ARMY
  casualties 170
  corpses in trench 96
  mutinies 181
  tanks 180-1
  trench warfare 96
  Verdun, Battle of 134-6, 173

French, General Sir John 49, 78

Fryatt, Capt Charles 140

fur jackets, government issue 92-3

G

Gallipoli
  Anzac Cove defence 108
  Anzac Cove landing 106
  description 78-9
  Helles attack 106
  landings 106, 107

gas attacks
  British advancing through gas 101
  British use 78
  British victims 260-1
  German use 77, 100-1

gas sentry 138

George V, HM King
  Cenotaph unveiling 283
  Derby Day 272-3

GERMAN ARMY
  advance post 207
  Aisne, Battle on the 207
  assault 243
  behind the lines, New Year's Eve 1915: 80-1
  casualties at Broodeseinde Ridge 222
  front line living conditions 91
  horse transport supply column 242
  infantry advancing 56-7
  machine-gun crew 146-7
  pre-war 18, 20-1, 22, 24
  reservists called-up 42
  trench warfare 70, 95, 122-3
  Verdun, Battle of 134-6, 171
  Villers-Bretonneux 244
  water bottle gesture 151

GERMAN ARMY CASUALTIES
  amputees 277
  dead soldier at Villers Devy Dun Sassey 268-9
  dead soldier near Havringcourt 224
  dead soldier near Ovillers 223
  dead soldier, First Battle of the Marne 63
  Meteren 256
  prisoners of war 113, 133, 148-9, 221, 236-7, 258, 266
  Verdun 171
  wounded prisoner of war 168-9

Germany
  civilians pre-war 18-19
  mobilization order 30

Gordon Highlanders 65, 90

"Grimsby Chums" 41

Guards Division 250-1

Guinchy. Battle of 162

H

Haig, General Sir Douglas 50, 77, 116-17

haircuts 164

Hamilton, Lt R G 106

Hindenburg, Field Marshal Paul von 51, 238

Hindenburg Line 180, 241

Hines, John "Barney", the "souvenir king" 220

Honourable Artillery Company 32, 94

horses, casualties 166-7, 230-1

I

Inniskilling Fusiliers 210

Irvine, Major F D 106

J

Joffre, General Joseph J C 49

K

Kaiserschlacht 238-9

King's Regiment (Liverpool Scottish) 98-9

King, Capt D M 106

Kings Own Scottish Borderers 109

Kitchener, Lord 79

L

Lancashire Fusiliers 144

Lancashire Regiment 97

Leicester Regiment 226-7

lice 50, 123, 127, 161

Lille 266-7

Liverpool Irish Regiment 266-7

LONDON
  armistice celebrations 271
  Bethnal Green family 279
  Buckingham Palace 119
  buses as troop transport 203
  Cenotaph unveiling 283
  coffee stall in Auchonvillers 176
  Hampstead, army training 84
  Hyde Park, WAACs drilling 188-9

Stock Exchange 28-9
  Victoria station 121
  Waterloo station 45
  Whitehall proclamation of war 31
  Zeppelin attack 104-5

London Regiment 84, 87

London Rifle Brigade 68

London Scottish Regiment
  survivors 66-7
  training 85

Loos, Battle of
  advancing through gas 101
  after the battle 102
  description 78

Ludendorf, General Erich 51, 238, 239-40

M

Marne, First Battle of the 49, 62-3

Masurian Lakes, Battle of the 51

Menin Road 218-19

Messines Ridge 181

Messines, Battle of 66-7, 210

Middlesex Regiment 62-3

mine chamber and mine explosion 142-3

Moltke, General Helmut von 49-50

Monchy-le-Preux 156

Mons, Battle of 49
  before the battle 58
  retreat from 59, 60

Moorhouse, Capt 67

Morval, Battle of 155

mules 217

N

Neuve Chapelle, Battle of, description 77

New Zealand army 258-9
  chaplain 195

Northumberland Fusiliers 132-3, 164

O

Operation Michael 238-9
Outbreak of the War 48
"Over the Hill" 102
Ovillers 223
Oxford and Bucks Light
   Infantry 64

P

Parfett, Ned 10-11
Passchendaele, Battle of
   239
   casualties 222
   description 181-2
Pilckem Ridge, Battle of 181,
   215-17
Ploegsteert Wood 68
Plumer, General Sir Herbert 77,
   181, 239
Princip, Gavrilo 27

R

railways
   light railway, Elverdinghe
      212-13
   tracklaying near Boesinghe
      210-11
rats 50, 122, 205, 246
refugees 46-7, 61
Reynolds, Sapper R 106
Roberston, General Sir William
   115
Royal Flying Corps 78
Royal Fusiliers 58, 150-1
Royal Garrison Artillery 141,
   196
Royal Marine Artillery 140
Royal Military College rugby
   match 186-7
Royal Naval Air Service 50
Royal Naval Division 108-9
Russia 50-1, 76, 182, 238

S

Saffron Walden army training
   85

St Eloi 94, 132-3
Schlieffen Plan 48-50
Scots Guards
   behind the front 69
   funeral December 1914: 73
Seabrook brothers 227
"shell crisis" 76
Siegfried-Stellung 180, 241
Smith-Dorrien, General Sir
   Horace 77
Soisson road 208-9
SOMME, BATTLE OF THE
   British artillery 140-1
   Canadian army 145
   casualties 117
   description 114-17
   fixing bayonets 144-5
   newspaper report 149
   opening barrage 139
   St Pierre Division 168-9
   Wiltshire Regiment 152
Suffolk Regiment 128-9

T

tanks
   Cambrai, Battle of 228
   first use 116
   French army 180-1
   versus tanks engagement
      239
   Vimy Ridge 192-3
Tannenberg, Battle of 51
Tardenois, Battle of 258
Templeux 242
Territorial Force pre-war 25
Thiepval 116
Titanic, newspaper seller
   10-11
trench warfare origin
   50-1
trench-foot 50
Tull, 2nd Lt Walter 130
Turkish army sniper 110

U

Unknown Warrior's coffin
   honoured in France 281

V

Verdun, Battle of 114, 134-6,
   171
   comparison with Hell 172
   unknown victim 172
Vimy War Memorial 282

W

WAACs drilling, Hyde Park 188-
   89
Wandsworth Regiment 86
War
   outbreak of 48
   "over by Christmas" 49, 51, 72
   "over by October" 38
water bottle gesture 151
Webster, Capt F A M 86
Westminster Fusiliers 45
Wiltshire Regiment 152, 160
Wood, Capt Derwent 274-5

Y

"Y" Wood Hooge 98-9
Ypres, First Battle of 64, 65
Ypres, Second Battle of 94, 96
Ypres, Third Battle of 210-11
Ypres, Third Battle of
   description 181-2

Z

Zulu troops, ceremonial
   performance 252-3

Picture Acknowledgements

Corbis; 32, 34-35, 39, 63, 91, 103, 104-105, 121, 122, 136, 151,167, 170, 171, 173, 180, 183, 186, 232, 233 top, 233 bottom, 238, 248, 256-257, 263, 264, 264-265, 266, 268-269, 278-279, 280, 281, 282, 283.

Courtesy of Doug Cheeseman; 130.

Getty Images; 10-11, 12, 13, 14, 16, 17, 26, 27, 31, 42, 51, 55, 59, 70, 74-75, 83, 85, 96, 118, 119, 145, 172,/AFP; 208-209, 218-219, 241, 244, 246, 270-271, 272-273, 279.

Imperial War Museum, London; 1, Q4502; **2-3;** **4-5,** Q3011; **6-7; 8-9,** Q777; **15,** Q81819; **28-29,** Q81729; **30,** Q81755; **36-37,** Q.30,067; **38,** Q90896; **40,** Q53581; **41,** Q53286; **45,** Q81781; **56-57,** Q.53446; **58,** Q 70071; **60,** Q.51200; **62,** Q.51489; **64,** Q.57205; **65,** Q.57258; **66,** Q.60737; **67,** Q.56210; **68,** Q.11,730; **69,** Q.57362; **71,** Q.70075; **73,** Q.57393; **76,** Q.30014; **79,** Q.13637; **82,** Q53929; **84,** Q.53596; **86,** Q53632; **87,** Q53832; **90,** Q.90287; **92-93,** Q.48957; **94,** Q.49369; **97,** Q.50418; **98,** Q.49750; **99,** Q49751; **100,** Q.48951; **101,** HU63277B; **102,** Q.60740; **102,** Q1122876; **107,** Q.99723; **108,** Q.13426; **109,** Q.70701; **110,** Q.13392, **111,** Q.13,622; **112-113,** Q.802; **114,** HU95895; **117,** Q.1071; **120,** Q.20048; **124,** HU95894; **127,** HU95893; **131,** Q.1062; **132,** Q.493; **133.** Q.496; **134-135,** Q.23760; **137,** Q.110; **138,** Q.669; **139,** Q.4066; **140,** Q.943; **141,** Q. 4867; **142,** Q.115; **143,** Q.756; **144,** Q.79490; **146,** Q.89; **147,** Q.87923; **148,** Q.79508; **149,** Q.79512; **150,** Q.777; **152,** Q3247; **153,** Q.4383; **154,** Q.1458; **155,** Q.1312; **156,** Q.23612; **157,** Q.4245; **158-159,** Q .1340; **160,** Q.1108; **162,** Q.1303; **162-163,** Q.1436; **164,** Q.1366; **165,** Q.1377; **166,** Q.7156; **168,** Q.4602; **168-169,** Q.4502; **176,** Q.4545; **177,** Q.1627; **178-179,** E.AUS 4599; **184-185,** HU95884; **187,** Q.54268; **188,** Q. 54089; **189,** Q.4673; **190,** Q.4642; **192,** Q.6229; **193,** C.O.1575; **194,** C.O.1636; **196,** Q.6460; **197,** Q.1994; **198,** Q.5095; **199,** Q.5102; **200-201,** HU95896; **202,** HU95899; **203,** Q.5238; **204,** HU95898; **205,** HU85892; **206,** HU95900; **207,** Q.55005; **210,** Q.5493; **211,** Q.5709; **212-213,** Q.2641; **214,** Q.7814; **215,** Q.5935; **216,** Q.5936; **217,** Q.5773; **219,** E.AUS 672; **220,** E.AUS 822; **221,** Q.3013; **222,** E.AUS 3684; **223,** Q.3991; **224,** Q.3182; **226,** Q.6279; **227,** HU93520; **228,** E.1413; **229,** Q.6341; **230-231,** Q.6041; **234,** C.O.2012; **235,** Q008382; **236-237,** Q.11329; **242,** Q.55226; **243,** Q.855483; **245,** Q.23679; **247,** Q.11578; **249,** Q.65895; **250,** Q.9187; **251,** Q.9188; **252-253,** Q.2388; **254,** Q.11250; **255,** Q.8077; **256,** Q.7928; **258,** C.O.11086; **258-259,** Q.11243; **260-261,** Q.011586; **261,** Q.72619; **262,** Q.31214; **266-267,** Q.9574; **270,** Q.3362; **274 Top,** Q.30449; **274 Bottom,** Q.30449; **275 Top,** Q.30456; **275 Bottom,** Q.30457; **276,** Q.33687; **277,** MH34196;

Max Arthur; 18-19, 20-21, 22-23, 24-25, 80-81, 95, 123.
Mirrorpix; 33, 43, 44, 52, 53, 54, 72, 88-89, 191, 195, 224-225.
Historical photographs of the Great War, Péronne (Somme) Courtesy of Musee Royal de l'Armee, Bruxelles; 61, 46-47, 48.
Taff Gillingham Collection; 125, 126, 128, 161, 174-175.

Author Acknowledgements

At Cassell Illustrated, I would like to thank Iain MacGregor, Publishing Director, who commissioned the book, and waited patiently for it to arrive; Joanne Wilson, who diligently collated the material and organised it for publication, Laura Price, who dealt admirably with the final draft and Steven Edney, UK Sales Marketing Director of Octopus Publishing Group for his support and enthusiasm.

I would also like to thank Alan Wakefield at the Imperial War Museum, and the rest of the very helpful staff, and Rachael Cross at the Wellcome Collection, Taff Gillingham for his photographs of the Suffolk Regiment and Gregor Murbach for finding the early shots of the retreat from Mons. Robert Waite of the Bruce Castle Museum was most helpful in finding the picture of Walter Tull. I would like to thank Mel Knight at Mirrorpix, and Warwick Woodhouse, who introduced me to Matthew Butson of the Hulton Archive, where Luigi DiDio gave invaluable assistance. My friend Dr Richard Danjic, whose remarkable collection of facial injuries from the Great War is unique, was immensely helpful.

Joshua Levine has been, as always, an enormous help with the book, as has Vicky Thomas. I am indebted to them both. I am also grateful for the support of Sir Martin Gilbert and my dear friend Ruth Cowan.